The Pterodactyl's Wing

The Pterodactyl's Wing

Edited by Richard Gwyn

PARTHIAN

Parthian
The Old Surgery
Napier Street
Cardigan
SA43 1ED
www.parthianbooks.co.uk

©The Authors 2003
All Rights Reserved.

ISBN 1-902638-28-X

Typeset in Sabon

Printed and bound by Dinefwr Press, Llandybie

With Support from the Parthian Collective

Parthian is an independent publisher that works with the
support of the Arts Council of Wales and the Welsh Books
Council

British Library Cataloguing in Publication Data.
A cataloguing record for this book is available from the British
Library.

Cover Design: Marc Jennings

We've nothing vast to offer you, no deserts
Except the waste of thought
Forming from mind erosion;
No canyons where the pterodactyl's wing
Falls like a shadow.

from R.S. Thomas *A Welshman to any Tourist*

Contents

xi

Richard Gwyn was brought up in south Wales and educated in London and Cardiff. He spent ten years travelling on and around the Mediterranean, with extended stays in Crete and Catalonia, forming enduring links with people, places and wooden boats. He has written five collections of poetry, a catalogue study of two contemporary painters, and has been involved in collaborations with visual artists in Wales, France and Spain. He has also been widely published as a critical commentator on issues relating to the body, health and communication. He is Poetry Editor of Parthian and teaches creative and critical writing at Cardiff University.

A Preface in Fragments

One fine day Edmund Plunkett, my great-grandfather, a Catholic from Portrush, County Antrim, set out to the furthest enclaves of the British Empire to look for gold. He was a mining engineer whose life ended abruptly at the age of 49 while leading a rescue team to recover trapped miners in a coal-pit in Chirk, North Wales. My Glaswegian grandmother (his daughter) kept a small glass cylinder of gold dust in her sitting room, the only record (apart from his parsimonious and horrifying journal describing a late colonial romp through Malaysia) of his magnificent failure. The glass container was of a shape and size perfectly shaped for a child's hands. As a small boy at primary school, I would go straight to this pot of fool's gold whenever I visited my grandmother's house in Llangenny Lane. I loved holding its heavy alchemist's bowl in my hands, fingering the slender corked stem, and conjuring stories from the snippets of information that my grandmother gave me; weighing up in my mind the possibilities involved in finding real gold rather than this blemished variety; asking how many of such pots would be needed to make a person wealthy, et cetera. Never satisfied with any of the answers I was given, what I really wanted to know was whether there was an element of chance in finding gold, or whether expert prospectors stood a better chance than anybody else, and since my great-grandfather had been some kind of an expert, how it was that he had failed. I remember this as being a source of puzzlement, one that stirred an indefinable sense of anxiety. Although my grandmother spoke of her father with reverence, he had obviously failed in a significant way. Put in other words, viewed through the lens of an adult's retrospection, I wondered, in a haphazard way, whether the pursuit of real gold might be an entirely serendipitous enterprise or whether it was easier to find real gold if you were expressly looking for it.

I choose to see this story partly as an allegory for the task of an editor; seeking out the specks of gold among the silt and rubble of the riverbed, but also because I love tales of failure, and of how the dreams of men (such as Edmund Plunkett) turn to rubble. Here, inside a bottle, was all that remained of the aspirations of one man. The tiny discoloured grains of his own odyssey of failure. It is appropriate then, that I begin this preface to an anthology of Welsh poets in another country, Catalonia, itself the object of colonization by a larger imperial power (or rather two imperial powers, since France too laid claim to it on occasion), but also a country itself implicit in the construction of Spain's monumental failure in the conquest and colonization of America. Catalans played their part in the colonization of the New World just as the Welsh, the Irish and the Scots all (though some of them pretend to forget this) were at various times willing participants in Anglo-Saxon claims to world domination. And our literatures reflect this: we are all hybrids of one kind or another, both colonized and colonizing.

*

An axiom of anthologies is that they tend to go out of date as soon as they are published (some are even out of date before they are published). If this is the case, then how much truer it is of the anthology's Preface. The Preface is, at the best of times, an ambiguous construct, perhaps, as Derrida has proposed, narcissistic, but of a particular brand of narcissism, "in which a proud parent looks upon and praises, excuses, or otherwise prepares the way for his child, the text that he has at once sired and given birth to."[1] Well, not precisely, at least not in this instance. We might consider, instead, the anthology preface as a text both in conflict with, but also reflective of, its own imminent outdateness.

A second axiom that we might consider is that every anthology is a compromise. By which I do not simply mean that a particular anthology cannot be representative of the totality of poets it claims to represent, but more, that the very fact of delimiting the anthology to certain poets, rather than including others, compromises, or distorts the nature of the enterprise from the start. This, of course, is inevitable, and usually involves the editor in a process of justification and explication; a procedure which to some degree seeks to pre-empt the criticisms of reviewers, who invariably home in on the inclusion of certain poets at the expense of others, and often seem more interested in what is not in the anthology than what is.

However, rather than jump in and start defending my selections and justifying my omissions, I'd like to provide some reflections on the background to this bizarrely titled project, and then later set about the business of defending and justifying. If none of this appeals to the reader, then you are advised to skip the preface and read the poems.

While this is an anthology of poets who are Welsh, either by birth, by adoption or by choice of residence, it is in no sense nationalistic. It is not an anthem to Welshness or to the increasingly irrelevant notion of national identity. The paraphernalia that surrounds that identity, however inoffensive or insipid (like the wearing of the daffodil) fails to inspire in me much beyond the gloomy memory of a lonely childhood and wet slate roofs. A daffodil is a daffodil is a daffodil. This obligatory and rather sad insistence on icons resonates, for me, with a distrust of anthems, flags and insular nationalism. By contrast, I am fascinated by borders, the liminal, the spaces between things, and intrigued by the vicissitudes of parenthood that allocate to each of us a particular cultural identity over and above any other of the hundreds available on this planet. Moreover, I don't feel circumscribed by my own mongrel identity: I prefer to see it as a springboard from which to dive into other waters. That is one of the things that poets are good for. They are, ideally, detached, as well as being a part of the things they detach from. They can lie for a profession, as Plato suggests, but their lies, or fabrications, contain, if they are lucky, a deeper truth than literal truth can ever muster. As Sallust reminds us: "These things never happened; they always are."

*

It seems pertinent that I am writing this in the study of a friend of mine who died four years ago, in a village in the Albera mountains, the final stretch of the Catalan Pyrenees before they meet the Mediterannean. The village has a population of 107. Within a few minutes walk from the house, I can be in one of the few remaining parts of western Europe that doesn't feel like either a shopping mall or a tidily conserved leisureland landscape. There is a fierce mountain wind blowing, the Tramuntana, and the corrugated plastic on the roof terrace is occasionally lifted off its bolts by a gust, and rattles with a deafening clatter. Something like a Pterodactyl attempting take off from a space too narrow for its wingspan, I would imagine.

I call Martin my friend, although I only met him three or four times. His family were originally from Pembrokeshire and he was an historian and translator. This study, which takes up most of the third floor of the house, is testimony to his intellectual eclecticism, as well as his personal dishevelment. Rows of books rest on sagging planks, held up by breeze blocks. The bare stonework has been hastily daubed in whitewash, which has splashed onto the timber above the window frames. The books cover poetry and prose fiction in English, French and Spanish; history, psychology, philosophy, cultural criticism and the flora and fauna of the Pyrenees. In one Spanish Encyclopaedia of plants that I dipped into, I was informed that the powerfully hallucinogenic Datura, or crabapple plant "grows abundantly and is not difficult to locate but will become so if you are expressly looking for it". An odd statement in an otherwise lucidly functional reference book. Of course, it set off a chain of reflections, terminating in my grandmother's living-room.

Here in this study then, is the potted biography of a man via his library, telling of his intellectual and spiritual quest. Manuscripts abound, loose in cupboards, spilling out of filing cabinets; identical pages from an unfinished novel, with revision upon revision pencilled in. A poem by Rilke above his computer called *The Machine*: "words will soften at what they can't say". Post-its posted to himself, still in place four years after his passing on. There is so much dust here that I haven't even attempted dusting. It would only encourage more dust.

Martin wrote a preface once. It opens his translation of Hurtado de Mendoza's *The War in Granada*, a sixteenth century account of the expulsion of the Moors from Andalucia in 1492.[2] The preface was a form ideally suited to Martin's discursive style. In fact his preface to Mendoza's book is a short masterpiece in the art of preface-writing, in which he unwittingly tells us almost us much about himself as he does about his subject.

It is tempting to consider Martin in conjunction with, or in counterpoint to, another son of Pembrokeshire: Waldo Williams, in many ways his antithesis. Waldo, a poet bonded, though never crowded in, by his sense of community and heritage. Certainly not a man given to restless wandering. Everything that Waldo needed was to be found within the confines of his native *bro*; a man who knew that "Earth is hard text to read" and resolved the issue by staying put.

Waldo then, resolutely finding his place in his little garden of eternity, and Martin, whose life served as an extended preface to the novel he never completed, thereby in some mysterious way rendering the novel itself redundant. And this life, upon which I am currently a retrospective voyeur, provides two lessons in the construction of a preface. First, that whatever you are ostensibly writing about often tells more about you, the author, than the subject matter, and second, that nothing is ever fully completed. Least of all a poem. Even less an anthology.

*

So to return to the volume you are (presumably) holding in your hand. I chose the title *The Pterodactyl's Wing* because I am in fundamental disagreement with R.S. Thomas regarding pterodactyls and canyons in the quote from *A Welshman to any Tourist* which prefixes this book. The idea that "We've nothing vast to offer you, no deserts/Except the waste of thought/Forming from mind erosion" presents a monstrously fatalistic vision. Now I can appreciate this image within a wider perspective, of a philosophical stance (albeit a perverse one for a priest). I can also see how, within the context of the mid-twentieth century, such an image was apposite, corresponding with the bleaker European perpectives of Beckett and Celan, for instance; but within the confines (if we choose to see them as such, which RST chose to) of a poetry of national identity, we might look towards Nazim Hikmet in Turkey, or Yannis Ritsos in Greece, two of the greatest poets of the twentieth century, both of whom suffered lifelong harassment, torture and imprisonment for their beliefs (unlike RST), but who never questioned the power of the human will to overcome loss and celebrate life.

It has occurred to me (and it is not an original theory) that the problem with Wales is that we did not suffer enough. Fortunately, post-devolution Wales offers a variety of ways out of the quagmire of self-recrimination, if we have the wit and sense of purpose to take advantage of the moment. At the current time, I happen to believe that many of us who write poetry in Wales have plenty to offer other than "the waste of thought/Forming from mind erosion". Dwelling on our interminable misery and downtrodden status is precisely the kind of ballast, which, as Beckett himself observed (writing on the power of 'habit') "chains the dog to his own vomit".[3] We in Wales have been habitually ingesting our own recycled vomit (or worse still, that of our powerful neighbour) for far too long. Some of us have even turned into the effigies of ourselves that those others have cobbled together from our own caricatures.

The image of Wales and the Welsh presented by R.S. Thomas, while undeniably 'true' in terms of his unique poetic vision, finds its counterpart in a more literal and ritualised form of self-denigration and pitiful self-obsession, (interspersed, sadly, by outbursts of inflated and jingoistic bombast, especially among our so-called journalists and members of the jockstrap cult). So, I suggest, as an alternative, bringing on the pterodactyls, and the canyons, and if you argue that we never had them, I will contest that we have, and that we do, for there are things that lie within the imagination (of which pterodactyls are only an example) that do not have to be carbon dated, nor grounded in a literalistic understanding of prehistory. What we make, is ours. The patterns we trace in the sand become the inheritance of our children. Accepting always that these things never happened and therefore cannot be, is no more than an entrapment: the dogma of literalism which is the enemy of poetry. As Octavio Paz has commented, for years (notably in the middle and latter parts of the last century) poetry was bound to this false sense of literalism. It had its wings clipped by those who would bomb us into extermination, cry damnation from the pulpit, or else sulk in the corners of fields and ruminate on sheep (the terminal metaphor of bad Welsh poetry). But their version of the world, the literal one, is just as much a fiction as any other. They never fooled us. These things never happened; they always are.

*

Back in Cardiff I live in Grangetown. Iwan Bala writes of the plurality of origins around him in his Grangetown home, Bengali, Somali, Hindu, Sikh, while 150 miles away his father has just come home from Chapel, inhabiting a world in which everything is carried out through the medium of Welsh. "Core identity" writes Bala "is undermined by global culture. It never seemed necessary for my father to define his identity. I seem to be constantly doing it".[4]

Multi-culturality, pluralism, acculturation. Globalization, both the bad kind and the good. Even the priest in this Catalan village managed to slip in a reference to globalization during his Epiphany sermon. An end to discriminatory categories. Nationalism of the small nations rising in direct response to the homogeneous constrictions of the nation state. And our Welsh nationalism, because it derives from a minority and sometime oppressed people must necessarily be different from and better than theirs. So we rightly support Irish and Scottish, Breton and Basque struggles for self-determination, but ridicule the rising spectre of English Nationalism. At times, too, we can imagine that all such nationalisms can be overriden in the new era of global culture, but the evidence points elsewhere. To what extent are we willing, or active, participants in this process of multicultural harmony? How easily do we slip back into our own corrugated folds whenever the threatening winds start to blow?

In a world that fetishises plurality and multiculturality at the same time as redefining the identity of smaller countries and the nation states that have engulfed them, in Fortress Europe at least, within the framework of an integrated alliance or federation, what is the significance of publishing a book of under-represented and sometimes unpublished poets, the majority of whom would identify themselves as 'Welsh', like myself, but for some of whom Wales is more a point of reference, or the place in which they have chosen to live? Perhaps the two issues are separate and distinct, but I suspect they are not. I suspect also that the idea of a postcolonial literature is one that merges with the aims of this book, although coming at it haphazardly, and from another direction.

Plurality, integration, multiculturalism. Who on earth knows who they themselves are in all this mess of movement, migration, tacit segregation and attempted acculturation? *It never seemed necessary for my father to define his identity. I seem to be constantly doing it.* We are all as malleable as the soil from which we came. And although millions of years have passed since the pterodactyls flew above the valley of Grwyne Fawr, we still receive light from stars which emanated while they were doing just that.

*

The original criteria for the anthology, while in the hands of another editor, and submitted to the Arts Council of Wales, were that contributors should not have had a volume of poetry published prior to 1985 and are not published by well-known English publishing houses. These criteria explain the exclusion of such fine writers as Robert Minhinnick, Gwyneth Lewis, Peter Finch, Tony Curtis, Duncan Bush, Nigel Jenkins, Stephen Knight and Oliver Reynolds, as well as our more senior poets such as Gillian Clarke, Dannie Abse, Tony Conran and others (the writing of this list makes one aware that there is certainly no dearth of talent among living Welsh poets). The other criteria were that they be 'younger' and/or 'under-represented'. Both of these criteria are fairly loose. Owen Sheers is young but hardly under-represented. At least three of our contributors produced volumes of poetry before 1985: Hilary Llewellyn-Williams, Landeg White and Chris Torrance. Of these, Landeg White is criminally 'under-represented' and Chris Torrance, while a well known figure in the so-called 'underground' press, is included (quite apart from his status as a poet) as a tribute to the seminal influence that his 'Adventures in Creative Writing' workshops had on an entire generation of budding writers, held at Cardiff University over many years. Several of the poets in this collection attended these workshops and his influence on poets from the not-so-young to much younger poets, is testimony to the excellence of that influence. Age is in itself not a worthy factor for inclusion or exclusion, since many poets begin writing (or at least publishing) much later in life than others, whose best work might be done in their early twenties.

And after reading your way through piles of manuscripts, how best to explain the sudden gleam of inner recognition as you begin reading the poems of a writer whose work you have not encountered before and which immediately hits a familiar throbbing vein. That recognition of otherness too, such as occurred when reading Rhian Saadat's sensuous word-tapestries, or sifting through Lynne Rees's mercurial poems (which appeared uninvited through my letterbox), or coming across the work of Landeg White and realising someone with five collections has somehow slipped through the British literary net unrecognized, despite his wonderfully lucid and evocative poetry. Somebody for whom the terms pluralism and multiculturalism were a reality long before they made the cultural studies hit parade and then became mangled by a neo-Thatcherite Labour government?

It is in response to the kind of poetry that I found most inspiring to read, which whetted my appetite for more, a poetry which, as André du Bouchet has written, "is nothing but a certain astonishment before the world and the means for this astonishment"[5], that the present selection eventually came about, and was subtitled with the 'Welsh World Poetry' epithet. Within that ambiguous and half-ironic phrase, suggested by Richard Davies at Parthian, we would hope to encapsulate the idea that while these poems are by Welsh writers, they largely represent an outward-looking Welshness, or at times an exile's view of Wales, written from beyond our borders and inciting a deeper reflection on what Welsh poetry is and might be. This vision is, I believe, one that has already begun to flourish during Robert Minhinnick's editorship of *Poetry Wales*, and it is due to his broader understanding of Welsh poetry within a world context that several of the poets in this collection have come to the attention of readers in Wales. But more, it is the only viable direction for Welsh writing, both in poetry and prose, to take. Otherwise we risk being incarcerated interminably into that colonial vision of ourselves furnished by others and perpetuated by ourselves.

*

Every poem is a Fiesta, Octavio Paz reminds us, and a Fiesta, apart from being a date in the calendar year "is also a break in the sequence of time and the irruption of a present which periodically returns without yesterday or tomorrow."[6] If a poem is a Fiesta, and we the readers are privileged guests, it is worth considering what precisely we are engaged in. The reading of a poem might be a break in linear time, an incursion of emotion or pathos or reflection, but it cannot be a passive process. It is not like settling down to *Hello!* magazine or the latest installment of *Eastenders* (or *Pobl y Cwm*). Similarly, editing an anthology is not simply a question of selecting poems and poets that you happen to like, since it is imperative in a book of this kind to give space to voices with which you disagree, that deliver versions of the world which you do not share, to include styles of writing you may even be hostile towards.

Part of the problem in making selections for the anthology lay in deciding to what extent we took into account the historical precedents of Welsh poetry, in both languages. Clearly, no anthology of Welsh poetry can be remotely representative if we exclude poetry in the Welsh language, and our original intention was to make this volume inclusive of contemporary poetry in Welsh. However, on being informed that such a volume is shortly to appear from Bloodaxe Books, we limited ourselves to the English language. But that is not to say that we have totally ignored our heritage in order to assert some faddish concern with a globalized, English language, vision of Wales. Shifting populations and changes in the balance of language choice have conspired over the past two hundred years to make much of Wales an English monoglot society. It is only by a phenomenal act of will, courage and dedication on the part of a handful of language activists over the middle and latter part of the twentieth century that we can now envisage a sustainable future for *y Gymraeg*. Whether or not this lasts remains to be seen: the effort has been made, and is continuing to be made, to conserve and promote the Welsh language as equal partner in a bilingual Wales. The infrastructure, as language planners might tell us, is in place. Whether the global sweep of English renders such a resurrection into a minor glitch, a hiccup in the eventual demise of Welsh, or whether the language continues its resurgence, current readers of this anthology will never know. But, for better or worse (I suspect for worse) the dominant language of literary consumption is English, and although there are fine poets writing in Welsh whose work could easily be accommodated within a volume defining itself as 'Welsh world poetry', it would seem, in a way, to be an act of tokenism to include translations of these poets in an overwhelmingly English language book. (Besides, there are arguments to be made for Welsh poets not wanting their work translated, as a recent statement by the poet Twm Morys makes clear).[7]

It is essential though, as Paz writes in his Introduction to an anthology of Mexican Poetry, that within any national poetry "all poetic activity feeds upon history, that is to say, upon the language, impulses, myths, and images of its own time, and likewise it confirms that the poet tends to dissolve or transcend the mere historical process."[6] So we might absorb and transcend, both at the same time. This is not so difficult; in fact it seems a perfectly reasonable expectation from any poet with an insight into his or her own culture. But it need not be done through propaganda and sledgehammer politicizing: it is, I believe, more appropriately realized through innuendo and suggestion, the sidelong glance, the unfinished sentence.

Finally, and crucially, it is not merely to incite some response to the nature of Wales and Welsh writing that this Preface has been written. Poetry is (among other things) also the haunting of the poet by an almost impossible nostalgia, the lexis and syntax of a collective cultural memory. It is relevant to all writers in all places, and reflects only incidentally upon the writer's own subjectivity. Paul Auster writes: "To wander about in the world . . is also to wander about in ourselves. That is to say, the moment we step into the space of memory, we walk into the world."[8] By walking out into the world, we can more truthfully envision ourselves.

I have heard it said that all human myths can essentially be reduced to two variants. In the first the hero, or protagonist makes a journey. In the other, they stay at home. We might once have achieved just as much by staying at home, but that is no longer possible.

Richard Gwyn
Cardiff
4th April 2003

References:

1   Jacques Derrida *Dissemination* University of Chicago Press, 1983
2   Diego Hurtado de Mendoza *The War in Granada*
    The Folio Society, 1982
3   Samuel Beckett *Proust* Riverrun Press, 1989
4   Iwan Bala 'Appropriate Behaviour' *Planet* 124, 1997
5   André du Bouchet *Carnets* 1952-1956 Plon, 1990
6   Octavio Paz 'Introduction to the History of Mexican
    Poetry' *Mexican Poetry* Grove Press, 1989
7   Twm Morys 'A Refusal to be Translated' *Poetry Wales* 38(3),
    2003
8   Paul Auster *The Invention of Solitude* Penguin, 1988

Acknowledgments

The poems in this collection, if previously published, first appeared in the following publications:

Tiffany Atkinson 'Paddling' first appeared in *Poetry Wales*, 'Taxi Driver September 2001' and 'Photo from Belfast' first appeared in *New Welsh Review*, 'Tea' first appeared in *The Daily Telegraph*, 'Umami' first appeared in *The Bridport Prize Anthology*; **Deborah Chivers** 'Heron' first appeared in *Reactions 2: New Poetry Anthology*, University of East Anglia, 'Instep' and 'Wings' first appeared in *Poetry Wales*, 'The Knowledge' first appeared in *New Welsh Review*; **Sarah Corbett** 'The Witch Bag', 'Black Crow Woman', 'Feast', 'Green Rose' and 'The Night Before Your Funeral' first appeared in *The Witch Bag*, Seren, 'Starfish' and 'Bitter Fruit' first appeared in *Red Wardrobe*, Seren; **Lyndon Davies** 'Whiteout', 'Icons', 'Tincture', 'Le Maudit Maudit', 'Domestic', 'The Space of Saying', 'The Banner', 'The Just' and 'Pilgrim 1 & 2' first appeared in *Poetry Wales*; **Alexandra Duce-Mills** 'electric sparks' first appeared in *New Welsh Review*; **PC Evans** 'The Definitive Farewell', 'A Short History of Lust', 'Prayer for Abercynon', 'Rest Bay', 'Ezra Pound 1943', 'I don't know your house', 'A Flight of Gulls', 'I do not have to...', 'When we were tired', and 'A Pumpkin Head' first appeared in *Headland*; **Cliff Forshaw** 'Buddhas of Bamiyan' first appeared in *Poetry Wales*, 'The Poet's Stick' and 'Bar Life' first appeared in *Seshat*, 'Sea Changes' first appeared in *Orbis*, 'Mazatecan Witch' first appeared in *Encyclopaedia Psychedelica*; **David Greenslade** 'Here's a Country' and 'Border' first appeared in *Burning Down the Dosbarth*, Y Lolfa, 'Village' first appeared in

Fishbone, Y Wasg Israddol, 'Craft Shop' and 'Bara Brith' first appeared in *Cambrian Country*, Gwasg Carreg Gwalch, 'Mandrel' first appeared in *Each Broken Object*, Two Rivers Press, 'Make Salt', 'We Lived Together' and 'In That Country' first appeared in *Weak Eros*, Parthian, 'Oranges' and 'Peas' first appeared in *Creosote*, Two Rivers Press; **Richard Gwyn** 'Memory of Drowning' and 'In the Palace' first appeared in *Being in Water*, Parthian, 'Arrival at Vilarig in a Storm' first appeared in *stone dog, flower red/gos de pedra flor vermella*, Cyhoeddiadau Cranc, 'Modes of Travel' first appeared in *Defying Gravity*, Red Sharks Press, 'September 20, 1989' first appeared in *One Night in Icarus Street*, Red Sharks Press, 'Camels Trotting' first appeared in *Walking on Bones*, Parthian, 'Lifting the Virgin' first appeared in *The Prose Poem*, 'New Year's Journey' and 'Hunger for Salt' first appeared in *Poetry Wales*; **Graham Hartill** 'Silver John' first appeared in *Poetry Wales*, 'Fever Wind' first appeared in *Turas*, Red Sharks Press, 'Ghost Dance' first appeared in *Angels of Fire*, Chatto & Windus; **Viki Holmes** 'Lantivet Boy' first appeared in *Poetry Wales*, 'Miss Moon's Class' first appeared in *sampler* #6; **John Jones** 'Stone Stable' and 'In the Hedgerow, Something...' first appeared in *Tilt*, Hartill, Hools & Jones: The Collective Press, 'Sedimentary' first appeared in *Scintilla*; **Patrick Jones** 'autumn eternal' first appeared in *Poetry Wales*, 'reach', 'father's day 2000' and 'christmas lights in january' first appeared in *fuse*, Parthian; **Hilary Llewellyn-Williams** 'Making Landfall' first appeared in *Scintilla*, 'Animaculture' first appeared in *Animaculture*, Seren, 'Ivy', 'The Sealwife' and 'Letter to my Sister' first appeared in *Hummadruz*, Seren, 'Steering by the Stars' first appeared in *Poetry London*; **Lorna Lloyd** 'Paris Taxidermists Shop', 'Spiderman', 'Granny's Glass Eye', 'Fly Trap' and 'Stargazers' first appeared in *New Welsh Review*, 'The Cracked Lighthouse Prism' first appeared in Planet, 'Puddles' first appeared in *Poetry Digest*; **Mike McNamara**

'Donald Brown's Grave, Christchurch' first appeared in *Folio*, 'Donald Brown's Grave Revisited' first appeared in *Orbis*, 'A Child's Brief Benediction' first appeared in *Overhearing the Incoherent*, Grevatt & Grevatt; **Tôpher Mills** 'Apron' was first published in *The North*, 'T.B.' was first published in *The Journal of Anglo-Scandinavian Poetry*, 'Dis is jest tuh say like' was first published in *Swimming in the Living Room*, Red Sharks Press, 'Never Fuhget Yuh Kaairdiff' was first published in *Poetry Wales*, 'Lavernock Point' and 'Last Swim in Empire' were first published in *New Welsh Review*; **Kate North** 'Bistro', 'My Life as a Weather Girl', 'Shoe' and 'Lying with Croeso' first appeared in *Poetry Wales*; **Pascale Petit** 'Remembrance of an Open Wound', 'The Flying Bed', 'Portrait of my Brother as an Endurance Runner' and 'Portrait of my Mother as Xipe Totec' first appeared in *Poetry Wales*, 'The Mineral Mother' first appeared in *Quadrant*, 'My Mother's Clothes' and 'Skins' first appeared in *Heart of a Deer*, Enitharmon, 'The Straight-Jackets', 'Embrace of the Electric Eel' and 'Self Portrait as a Yanomami Daughter' first appeared in *The Zoo Father*, Seren; **Steve Prescott** 'Plastering' first appeared in *New Welsh Review*, 'The Bigger Picture' first appeared in *The Bristol Slam Anthology*; **Lynne Rees** 'White' and 'Teaching a Chicken to Swim' first appeared in *Iron*, 'Moving On' first appeared in *New Welsh Review*, 'Like Water' first appeared in *Poetry Ealing*, 'The Snow Queen' first appeared in *Orbis*, 'Visitors' first appeared in *Magma*, 'Ripe Fruit' first appeared in *Seam*, 'The Time Stealer' first appeared in *Rialto*, 'Cold' first appeared in *Reactions 2: New Poetry Anthology*, University of East Anglia; **Lloyd Robson** extract from 'letter from sissi' first appeared in *letter from sissi*, blackhat, extract from 'speed diary' first appeared in *Edge Territory*, blackhat, 'sandinista tequila tabasco' first appeared in *Red Poet's Society,* #7, 'get over it get down to it...' first appeared in *bbboing! & associated weirdness*, Parthian; **Cecilia Rossi** 'Speaking in

Tongues' and 'Mirroring Narratives' first appeared in *Poetry Wales*; **Rhian Saadat** 'Passing Through' first appeared in *Poetry London*, 'Sequoia', 'Table of Orientation', 'Weavers', 'Voyage of Discovery', 'Chez', 'Silk Route', 'Being Lost – Stage Five', 'Hall of Mirrors', 'Camel Deal' and 'Larger then Life' first appeared in *Poetry Wales*; **Owen Sheers** 'The Blue Book' first appeared in *The Blue Book*, Seren, 'Not Yet My Mother' first appeared in Poetry Wales, 'Unfinished Business' first appeared in *The 2001 Forward Book of Poetry*; **Zoë Skoulding** 'Trans-Siberian' and 'Tailor of Ulm' first appeared in *Poetry Wales*, 'Adela's Elephant' first appeared in *Poetry London*, 'The Aztec's of Cwm Llan' first appeared in *Planet*, 'Feathers' first appeared in *Magma*; **André Stitt** 'Substance' and 'November Night, Oporto' first appeared in *Homework*, Krash; **Ifor Thomas** 'My Recurring Nightmare is Trigonometry' first appeared in *New Welsh Review*, 'Llawhaden', 'When Your Wife Suspects' and 'Kiss' first appeared in *Poetry Wales*, 'What to Say When' first appeared in *Yellow Crane*, 'Post Christmas Drink' first appeared in *Christmas in Wales*, Seren, 'Weather Forecast' first appeared in *Unsafe Sex*, Parthian, 'Blocking Signals to the Heart' first appeared in *Roundyhouse*; **Chris Torrance** 'The Least Likely Buddha', extract from 'The Slim Book' and extract from 'Angel Busted' first appeared in *Poetry Wales*; **Landeg White** 'Incident at a Poetry Reading', 'Cotton, Rubber, Tobacco, etc', 'Chimwalira', 'Words for Heroes Days, Perhaps', 'For Her Wedding' and 'Charcoal' first appeared in *The View from the Stockade*, Dangeroo Press, 'Obituaries', 'Self Praises', 'Bacalhau' and 'Let Me Tell You Jack' first appeared in *South*, Cemar, 'When Paul Celan Met Heidegger' first appeared in *Poetry Wales*; **Samantha Wynne-Rhydderch** 'The Hunt' first appeared in *Poetry Wales*, 'First Aid Class', 'Willow Pattern', 'Pére Lachaise', 'Report', 'Blackshaw Head in the Wind', 'Paramilitary Lover', 'The Café Excelsior, Monatmartre',

'The Truth About Escalators' and 'Rowndio'r Horn' first appeared in *Rockclimbing in Silk*, Seren.

David Greenslade

Here's a Country

Here's a country
small enough
near enough
we can
shove our fingers in
and make it squeal
no one will ever know
not even
the body itself
conforming by word
and yield
to the probing
of our roads
our franchises
our newspapers
replacing its thoughts
with our legislation
its obedience with
our demands
its future with
our memory
its compliance
with our lust
here's a country
as dignified
as a fearless child
we can reduce it to the
degradation of a pornographic
baby
bringing it news
of our conquests

the indulgences of our King
rewarding it
with grants and
the breathing space
of schools subsidies
and special events
here is a country
close enough small enough
it can live
with all we cram into it
until it bursts
like a haemorrhage
and then we mop it
from the walls.

Border

You can't go in there
you won't like it
the country's all swollen up
bloated over-excited
exploding in civic blotches
scenic parades
there are screams groans
anthems marches
undignified complaints
if you already lived there
we wouldn't mind but
they're finishing the long job off
putting an end to all this
Cambrian nonsense it's time
for some brutal honesty
time to keep things
exactly as they are
while there's still some heat

some expiring breath
some traces of froth
in the Celtic Twilight
Welsh Arts Council
anthologists and the
Welsh Union of Writers
want a final solution
poets in Penarth and
Ogmore-by-Sea
fresh from their awards
are sponsoring the
Cardiff Festival
praising the dead breasts
of their grandmother's body
the names she once put
to familiar things
hiring staff to study her
perspective
this thread runs through
the country like a finger print
unless you were a visitor
you wouldn't notice anything
even then the disease you catch
depends on the malice of your host
we can't let you in
you expect too much
you want to know how
a self-respecting
people can live like this
swallowing ratlike amounts of
patronage
if you already lived there
you wouldn't see
but you are a curious visitor
and for our sake
we can't let your sort in.

Village

She is a new wife and he is showing her around. Each
description becomes more incredible. His mother choked
in the rugby club. His son committed murder. She buried
all her children. She was locked away until her husband
died. No one in their family ever looks at me. He deserted.
He is the oldest man in Wales. She stole the Sunday
School fund. He rose from the dead. She was born from a
speckled egg. They are soft jewels in the crown of his,
"Good morning!" He grows tired and longs never to be
described. His body shrinks, becoming one filthy sponge
drinking from the gutter of his childhood. The sobs of his
observations blacken with the cooking oil of a million
hurried meals. Now he is a pair of detached, hypnotised
feet. Two boys gaze into this marvellous pair of shoes, but
an electromagnetic force prevents anyone else from
wearing them. The sponge swells – heavy with gravy,
blood and water. The thirsty wife presses it against her
lips. She spits him out against a wall. They continue with
their tour of the village.

Craft Shop

This is the graveyard. Tranquilisers fixed and frozen,
decided into swollen cubes – convenient but cold and
angular to swallow. Where Blarney laps Efnisien's shore.
Here political stockings all fall down and the fancy
costumes of conditional suffrage and appropriated
heritage are finally the naked penny's own. Whispers that
have run out of wax. No one forced the shop to become a
counterfeit note in its own town. Whom do these useless
algorithms serve – making a fool of any sort of choice?
Inventory of antiquated lard in an age of pressed
rehabilitation. Whose over-polished glass beads were they?

Whose milk-dipped sops? Vague shapes passing through the dislocatable jaw, into the till's reptile gullet. Where, disguised as trade, they are better recognised for what they always meant to be. Takings. Anything, at the end of a retail visit on a tour of classified tokens. Merchants showed Sinbad how they took a lump of meat – sometimes the body of a slave – and hurled it at the end of ropes down into the canyon, hauling up precious stones embedded into it. These shops are lumps of meat.

Bara Brith

Imagine this: picking strawberries in a field near Valencia. The red, heavy, heart-shaped drops wait for your patient hands under their decoy of thick, furry leaves. As your small blue plastic box fills up, a flock of pink flamingos passes overhead. She is as surprised as you are. When she comes to stand next to you, she puts a strawberry in your mouth. When you are half way through eating it, she reaches up and kisses you. Later, at your favourite place in Wales, you go out with a flask of coffee in the evening. About an hour before the time of day when bats start to stir their wings, the nearby stream carries shadowed light quickly away under the sandy roots of deep, eroded banks. You have made two small loaves of bara brith – the colour of oak leaves still thickly clustered on the early autumn trees. Thrushes start to sing. It is so quiet you can hear blackbirds grubbing about between the withering brambles and feathery October grass. You cut the bread, pour coffee and pass them back and fore. You know the bats and snipe by their differently determined erratic bursts of flight. The speckled bread is moist and sticky. When she is half way through eating it, you lean across and kiss her.

Peas

Peas. Knuckle dusters. Ever worn a set? Boxing gloves.
Ever shelled a pod? Cut a peastick? In your face. Crazy
all the time. That's peas! Coming on strong; bursting at
the seams; trying to run the government; held back by
lousy bits of constitutional string. Why should they
forgive? Or dry up their tears? It's their depression; their
turn of phrase; their pregnancy. That's how they do
things. They'll talk to who the hell they like, and suffer
the consequences, whether we approve or not. How do I
know? When I was eight they spoke to me. What did
they say? They said, "You stay out of this. We're peas,
this is our way." I've never forgotten that.

Oranges

When there are oranges at home we feel secure. Or is it
paranoid? Screen upon screen of monitors. Well placed
cameras, as unpredictable as seeds, now at a traffic
junction, now at the striptease nightclub. Limitless
circumference, or so we thought, until suddenly the flesh
of the universe can, after all, be measured. Sometimes,
when the fuses blow, during a powercut, or camping, I
grope for Rhind's Vegetable Kingdom in the middle of the
night. I cut an orange in half and read by the glow of its
cellular moon. Oranges illuminate. The Moors in Spain
cultivated miniature citrus arboreta planted in the shape
of constellations. In Celtic countries, on January 1st, small
children still walk with oranges from door to door, as
though the orange were a torch shining into the year
ahead. If only this were so. Don't take my word for it.
When was the last time you sharpened a keen steel edge
on a kitchen knife? When there are oranges at home we
feel secure. Some of us. That why oranges are angry. No
matter what they give, it's never enough. Take take take,
that's all they get. And they don't get enough of that.

We lived together

We moved stones
to the edges of our field,

sleeping outdoors in summer.

The sky dense with stars,
the horizon dark

with other voices singing.

We lived together a long time,
sometimes weeping as we ate,

silent as we dug the garden.

I have known finding
and losing her,

both were terrible.

We shared black sand,
many fallen roses,

losing our portion of sleep.

David Greenslade

In That Country

In that country
currency was minted
in the shape of keys.

Shoes were
a flimsy bank.

I could take a coin,
turn it
in the ankle
of a beautiful woman,

opening her foot
like an orange
when it meets the frost.

I was a master thief.
I was always poor there.

Mandrel

Although you love the object
and display it – treasuring
its smooth collapse –
no one presses
its dark window or lights
their lamp to look for you.
It is a collier's mandrel. When
you clipped it to the wall,
polishing it as though your past
were now an information pack,
no hooter wailed its long wake

between slow verses of the shaft's
orchestral song. Instead, an old hand
reached up from the coal and, pushing
at your dust free breast, firmly
said goodbye to you.

Symptoms

I was retrieving
a small elastic band
from the heap of dishes
on my draining board
when I saw it again;
a little bit rising
from the tips
of the ring and index fingers
of my right hand.
I was definitely smouldering.
I went to the bathroom mirror
and saw smoke coming from
my right elbow, a trace
of it around my shoulders.
Urine – pale brown.
I check the bed – scorched.
Check my shoes – they smell of ash.

Make Salt

Where you sleep
    steers its dark wake to me.
    I've watched you groom
        sheer lust,
                fencing hours
        with your fingertips.
we've danced
        each   un-
                    strapped
            shoulder,
    forced
        our sleeping hips
                awake;
brewed pungent words,
        helped your white hair
            unspill;
your want-determined tongue
        climb towards
        my own astonished mouth,
        no breeze stirring,
        until the night tastes hot
            and we lick
                a gleam of moonlight
        from the drying racks.
"Dart!" you say.
"Make salt!"
            When morning
            cools our cloudy sheets
        a fine sting
scalds you.

Landeg White

Charcoal

There is a moment when the wood has caught
and the charcoal has done its tinkling
and glows lasciviously, when
the carafe of *Dão* or *Quinta da Bacalhoa*
simmers in our talk
of long delayed summers peering
down at long last down
our well between the terraced houses
north north north
on our tiles and towel of lawn,

there is a moment when the fumes of burning
lamb with oreganum, bay leaves and onions,
drift across the rag of lawn
to the brick wall where I'm reading
Walcott or Sebastião da Gama
or Dafydd ap Gwilym slagging
January, purring over May
and his burning trysts
in the improbable holly bush,
at that moment all our summers merge

in a scent so quick I don't know
what I'm remembering but, before
reductive words, happiness
floods, stinging my eyelids,
and I walk to where you are turning
skewers and I hold
your waist while you press
my wrists with your elbows:
all summers with wine and charcoal
are dark with south and south is you.

Landeg White

Incident at a Poetry Reading
(for Eduardo White, *primo*)

In the old walled garden the young poets
have spread laden tables under the mango tree.
We stand reverently in the starving city

eyeing the roast suckling pig, samousas,
fried prawns, chicken with groundnut sauce,
goat piri-piri, wines and beers,

while the speech from the dais about the young
poets' aspirations reaches its peroration
in a *caldeirada* of revolutionary slogans,

and we clap, our hands straining to do
what they do next, reaching out for food
and drink until all the tables are cleared

and we stretch our legs under the mango tree,
a black silence in the glistening sky,
enjoying the young poets' newest poetry.

Eduardo is long-limbed. He bears signs
of his mother's tenderness. His sudden
manhood has tightened like a skin.

His poem is angry. The nation is a neglected
garden rank with rotting fruits. Corruption
and our silence are forfeiting victories.

We watch him touched on the shoulder
by uniformed men. He falters in his reading:
detention without trial has its own prosody.

But "talk!" they insist. "You are telling truths,"
and the poem ends wildly with kisses and applause
and the evening in an afterglow of pleasure,

beer bottles clinking in the mango tree's shadow,
talk about language and the international standard,
tiny green mangoes dropping on our bare heads,

while beyond the *bairros* past the airport road
despairing peasants flock to the city for food,
and the siege tightens with mutilation and murder.

Chimwalira

The truth is he was born at Chimwalira
not Bethlehem. For Immanuel the conception
was a good one. But it was hard in a place
without writing to show prophecies fulfilled.
She gave birth on a reed mat in a mud house,
but so did every woman. How much grander
a stable signifying property in the foreground.
So when the Magi appalled by the Nile's
green wilderness turned back worshipping
a Jewish boy in a safe colony, they missed
their star's conjunction with Crux Australis
and God lay forgotten in Africa.
                              Chimwalira,
"where someone died". He grew up ordinarily,
neither Tarzan nor Shaka, eating millet
and wild mice. After his circumcision
there were songs about his dullness with women.
He became a blacksmith and a doctor skilled
in exorcism, and people saw he was touched.
But there was nothing startling to the elders
in his proverbs. He died old at thirty-three,
a normal life span.
                    (It was the Reverend Duff McDuff
screamed the Python priest was the Black Christ
as they led him to his steamer in their straightjacket.)

For her Wedding She Wore her Breasts Bare

For her wedding she wore her breasts
bare with woven beadwork at her waist
and plaited beadwork in her hair.
The girls sang, begging her
never to leave them for the bridegroom's mat.
Her heart soared as they drew her to his hut.

In Leeds she wears a duffle coat and headscarf.
Her straightened hair is shielded from the rain.
Her husband at the Poly studies husbandry.
He is proud his village wife wears dungarees.
She pushes her packed trolley round Tesco's,
black, pregnant, angry, missing

cowdung smouldering in the soft dusk as
cattle praises echo from the kralls.
The woodsmoke curls from cooking fires.
The children demand stories
or a lick of the ladle. Darkness drops.
The men come home in blankets with their pipes.

Words for Heroes' Day, perhaps

Being in the Welsh style uninclined to give politicians
credit for the brilliant acts their speeches enjoin us
to applaud on their tightrope strung between banks,

nor finding congenial the climate of cenotaphs,
rituals of death as though death were sacrifice
and sacrifice legitimised those hierarchies of stamping,

not being, in short, in any sense *imbongi* or praise poet,
whether sweeping thorns from the ruler's path or brandishing
a symbolic knobkerrie as spokesman for the people,

I am in the English manner a little at a loss to find
words for this anniversary when visiting after Empire
I am asked to pay tribute to those who died for Freedom.

That some were heroes is quite certain though not
necessarily the men on the platform (nor necessarily men).
Even the dead are ambiguous. Remembering them I think

most of those innocents cremated in their hundreds
as fire rained on the camps where they were queuing for flour.
Calling them heroes makes their slaughter seem called for

though their ghosts cry out for an eternal flame of anger.
Even among the warriors there were, as we too well understood,
the psychopathic who will never settle to justice.

But though irony has no heroes there is a poetry of facts.
There were others (not necessarily the men on the platform)
who are already legend and their legend a gracious one,

speaking of pastoral, the column filing through the tall
grass to a clearing with huts in the hut-high millet
and a shining welcome from the old who remembered the Rising,

speeches, courtesies observed with prayers to the ancestors,
songs and dancing, the girls crazy with admiration,
the meal from a shared pot when even a bean was divided,

then at moonrise moving onwards to the dawn's target,
and though doubting whether half of this happened or whether
half of that half matters in the unchanged city,

I honour them for the metaphors they died for. That
they made strutting ridiculous, if only momentarily,
is sufficient for our homage. May their ghosts

snatch at these anklets rattling today for our applause.

Cotton, Rubber, Tobacco etc

"So now you are going to have your coffee?"
says the interpreter approvingly,
and the villagers gather in a noisy circle to study
the white man drinking his coffee.

They have all grown coffee for the white man
and can tell me about every stage
of the culture and preparation – except for the drinking
which is hilarious to watch.

Who knows? Next I might change my underpants,
blow up a condom, burn
a cigar, or do something else they have worked
lives for and never earn.

Self-Praises

(for my African age-mates)
I climbed the old elm tree and read *William* books in the
rook's nest,
My knee stuck in the pulpit rail: for once the congregation
laughed,
The missionary told of the poison ordeal: I was spellbound
in the cub hut,
I won the match by slicing a six off the back of the bat over
backward point,
I cycled a hundred miles precisely to Nettlebed and back to town,
I planted crotons, a whole hedge in thirty-two varieties,
I scored Sparrow's *Melda* for the steelbands' *Panorama*,
I made love to the circuit-minister's wife in a dark corner
of the canefield,
I decamped from the island under an arch of leaping dolphins,
Baboons jumped on my steaming bonnet as I stalled on the
escarpment,

I crossed the longest bridge at dusk, reading of another country,
I found her on a sand dune where a coconut palm strained
at its bole,
She to whom all metaphors return was outlined with chevrons,
She stretched like a tigress, adorned with her stripes,
I watched the Beetle spinning downstream, swept from the
flooded causeway,
My dugout parted the hyacinths in search of the hidden history,
When the armed guerrillas ambushed us, I said *Oh, there*
you are,
From four jobs I resigned,
From the fifth the President deported me, without rhyme
or explanation,
I helped at my son's birth: he came out looking dumbfounded,
My proudest expedient, bribing our baby on to the plane!
The professor rang at midnight: my poem was a masterpiece,
I designed and built a kitchen to a millimetre's calculation,
I knuckled down to fifteen years of mortgages and pension,
I campaigned for my dear friend to step forth like Lazarus,
My vine, in Viking territory, was a miracle of survival,
My garden exploded in poppies and cornflowers: autumn
blazed in nasturtiums;
He wrote marvellously of his resurrection: it was I gave the
writing space.
They shook hands, enemies to the vein,
They shook hands and reminisced across my conference table
(The student wrote: *thank you, who else could we have got*
drunk with?).
As a scholar, I set the paradigm: as a poet I found my niche.
Let these praises float from my window, setting fires where
they will.

Landeg White

Obituaries: Up an' Under

21 January, aged 43, Countess 'Titi' Wachtmeister
  6 February, aged 83, William Younger GC
Model and sometime companion to Peter Sellers
  Hero of the Louisa Colliery disaster when 19 men
Along with King Gustav and ex-Beatle George Harrison
  Died in the blast or from snorting firedamp
(Condemned as 'vulgar' by the Crown Estates office
  He was at the coal face with two fellow deputies
When he tried to re-name his nightclub 'Titi's'
  And before midnight explosions wracked the seam).

Titi, with the looks of a blonde Jean Shrimpton
  But Younger knew all the shafts and roadways
A successful cover girl when she burst on London
  And ignored danger, clambering to the scene through
Parties and diplomatic modelling and society balls
  Derailed tubs and galleries choked with dust
Where Ben Ekland, Brit's brother, introduced Titi
  His canary dead, his lamp glowing barely a foot,
To Sellers, still married to Lord Mancroft's daughter
  And wrestled with his colleagues for almost two hours
Igniting a passion, despite their age difference,
  To move the injured and dying to a safer drift
But it ended in a wrangle over a Cartier watch
  Enabling five miners to be stretchered to the surface
Along with Titi's jewels and a favourite stuffed dog.

Gossip predicted marriage to King Gustav, but Titi
  Awarded the George Cross for gallantry
Wed Enrico Monfrini, a Geneva-based corporate lawyer
  Younger, modest and self-depreciating
The wedding attracted 150 jet setters
  After almost half a century in the pits,
Including Gunter Sachs and Dai Llewellyn

A grieving widower with two proud daughters
But a plumper Titi emerged from her separation
   Embodying the staunchness of the mining community
With a line of high-priced T shirts called 'T-T's Ts'
   (He bore his failing predicate with great courage).

(adapted from *The Times*, 10 February, 1993)

Bacalhau

1.
Another restaurant in Alcabideche! People
keep asking, *where's the new restaurant?*
and Alice directs them
confidently without having seen it.

Restaurants in Alcabideche are like
chapels in Wales. There is always some
new delicate doctrine
involving fresh coriander and salt cod.

At Christ's birth, codfish loom
on our TVs, glottal as Pavarotti,
roaring *Hark the herald* etc.
(The turkeys wilt and swoon.)

2.
Bacalhau again! I found it
in Soho, but 'it comes
from Hull' said Luigi, his
moustache quivering
at the absurdity: 'they send
the heads to Portugal.'

I hugged it under my elbow,
a brown paper rugby ball

in a neat net of string,
and set off across London.

At the F.O.
they were bombing Libya.
'One moment, sir'.

'It's *bacalhau*,' I said.
'Sir?'
'Salt dry cod.'

Gingerly, he weighed the device,
gave it a gentle wobble,
smelt it and held it to his ear
listening to the music of the seas.

'Salt. Dry. Cod, sir?'
'They send the heads to Portugal
under the Treaty of Windsor'.

He kissed the air and a dog,
special breed, tall
as the hat stand ambled
from the office, taking control.

My casket was offered knee high
like myrrh or frankincense
and I thought of the hundred recipes
simmering in the brown egg

   - *bacalhau*
     in the glorious names
  of Bulhão Pato, Gomes de Sá,
Batalha Reis. António Lemos,
Zé do Pipo and Brás.
   - *bacalhau*
     with cheese, with onions,

with potatoes and spinach,
with milk, rice, leeks, oysters,
parsley, prawns, flour with egg white
- *bacalhau 'with everything'*
   in the peasant style
with carrots
in the manner of heaven,
in twists like a corkscrew,
from Trás os Montes
   Guarda, Porto,
     Lamego,
       Ericeira,
         Alentejana, even
the despoiled Algarve,
and our winter favourite
  - *bacalhau que nunca chega,*
   'the cod that's never enough' –

I watched them hatching in the dog's
nostrils, clamouring
to spawn in the cold seas
of their birth.
      (Ghadafi'd
have surrendered on the instant,
adding his own touch
of tabina and walnuts.)

The Alsatian took a quarter sniff
turning its tail contemptuously.
Cook, poet, comedian,
I was harmless.
Our government's in safe paws.

(Alice White faults this poem for not including *Bacalhau á moda da Guida*, as prepared by Margarida Maria da Cruz Mergulhão of Casal Verde, Figueira da Foz.)

Let me tell you, Jack ...
(for, and after Jack Mapanje)

Let me tell you, Jack, what's beyond the veranda
Where I write most days, except when the north wind
Blasts from York across Biscay to ravage
Our pottery garden of the plants you know from home
- Hibiscus, elephant ears, Mary's milk, *piri-piri.*

I've lost count of the half poems launched to probe
For metaphors to enshrine what's out there. *Enshrine!*
Don't giggle! Obsolete words, like *enamelled*
Or *the painter's palette,* invade them for colours no one
Younger than 50 in England has ever exclaimed at!

And you know well enough I don't just observe
From a height. I'm down there daily, like Wordsworth
In the gap between stanzas, peering short-sightedly
At silks thrusting from the earth, and interrogating
Passers-by for the word, though they often don't know.

So my diary is of distances, of fragments and hesitations,
About white walls daubed with laundry and geraniums,
About the moss-green valley, where nettles even in winter
Surge knee-high, and snakes fat as pythons coil in the sun.
Pine trees cast shadows blacker than Alentejo bulls,

And spring's sequence of flowers is like a carpet somehow
Lit from within, changing not by the month or the week
But hourly between daybreak and noon and dusk
As the massed gold or china-blue or tortoiseshell petals
Open, revolving with the blossoming sun, and fold and decline.

I watch the cat boxing her kittens. Boys yelp like peacocks.
Cocorico happens too often to be any use as a clock.

Oh, but laugh at this! Our morning parade, as housedogs
Walk their mistresses, each circumscribed by her territory
Marked by a tree, a lamppost, and a raised hind leg.

You would hardly know the Atlantic is just a kilometre
Off, until the stump of a hurricane howls from New York
And the rain clouds scud like caravels, their hulls
Careened by the moon. Skies are important here, stars
In their consternations, flagging imperial destinies,

So I use you as reference point, your well being differently
Based, knowing our love (another jaded word, with its
Dangerous afterlife) will survive this latest exchange
Of countries and poems. This valley beyond my veranda
Is my newest mystery, my second-hand Brazil,

Where I'm less ex-patriate than in York. Out there
Between the almond trees and blue-black cypresses
Is a field of flowers where the Angolans are playing football.
Language will come. I want to continue living
Where I will always marvel at precisely where I am living.

Landeg White

When Paul Celan Met Heidegger

When Paul Celan met Heidegger
in that Black Forest hut

where the philosopher and nature met
in the manner of soiled centuries,

his question hung in the damp air:
what of Jews and the Gypsies?

Blue-eyed Hitler, vegecologist,
anti-smoker and folklorist,

concentrated all wanderers
and earthed them in his fires.

Such was the poet's right to ask
the philosopher was silenced,

and it echoes whenever a plot's
patrolled, *viz.*, what

of refugees, aliens,
asylum-seekers, Palestinians?

Celan found beautiful sport in the orchid.
I write in praise of the canine hybrid

that claims its space by hoisting
a leg, no matter who planted the lamppost.

Lyndon Davies

Druid's Altar
The Son

You can wait all day for the heron,
it's going to shock you anyway – clattering out
from the very alder-clump you most suspected
of harbouring what, at that time, in no way
resembled anything that could terrorize the leaves

or tear that yelp from your chest. It's necessary
to concentrate all day on the one thing,
but fail at it; for your greed to falter,
if only for an instant: say, when the cat jumps up
for the fly, or the phone goes, or that opalescent lustre

under the great magnolia tree seems suddenly grey,
unappetizing even, bringing to mind the dead,
who wait all day in their beds, but are not waiting
for anything really – the heron has already burst
from their tree. They have learned to live with it, as you

must now.

White-Out
Cora Sandel

Everything I needed to say about the snow
eludes me now: every clause, each adjective,
frost-ravaged, chafed to the bone, is white
on white. The snow keeps coming and the bones
are buried deep as the celandine, as the lark's flight.

I couldn't see what I needed to see
on waking. A lustre broods on the gloom;
its thin, devotional glimmer pervades the room
and consecrates the ceiling. This is a light
which strands: the shame of the wardrobe turns from the
                                        shame of the tallboy.

Snow blocks the doors and divides the villages:
each separate wish in its separate reliquary.
I lie in wait for the dawn, for the smell of coffee
to open the cloaca, to spill its guts.
The rosary of the breath counts out its beads.

Icons
Andrei Tarkovsky

I have lit the furnace, I have poured the metal
for the great bell. Now the water flows
over everything:
in the room abandoned for a very long time,
it flows through the rubble, covers it. Though it's just

a scrim, though it's just a wafer of impoverished light,
the water glides through the room, slides over
whatever has fallen there: bricks, laths, plaster,
pieces of cloth, leaves, photographs; and the voices
are in their element – they have found the weight

they needed to carry them down to the bottom,
down, far down, to the streambed, where the bell mouths
to the shadow, to where the furnace hungers
for the praise of the great hour, in the silent parish
which the water covers up, covers up and reveals.

Tincture
S.T.Coleridge

Dumbstruck, I struggled out from that mêlée,
clutching the single rose, in spite of everything –
blight, apathy, contusions – there it was in my fist
(locked tight for punching, probably; or for playing
that game – what is it? Something to do with potatoes).

I stumbled into the living room, clutching the bloom
that was going to prove my journey, to second it
in the eyes of the upright. O my god that upright,
legible and reliable citizen – there he was, looking on,
with his sour wit and his haemorrhoids.

He could have taken it from me as a gift,
from the mulch below the monolith – that most decorous,
stern watchtower. It might have been of use:
as a kind of landscape, possibly; a panorama
fit for rambling over, fit even for remarking upon.

Montgesty
The Sage

The worst thing, the very worst thing that could happen,
will happen to me. This makes me merry,
climbing the steps to the conical tower
in which the blue fly buzzed, though the fly
is gone, long gone.

It makes me merry
to hear the fly buzz in the conical tower,
and shouts from the swimming pool. The worst thing
that could ever have happened
happened before I got here.

Light from the pool sways up, the vortex
wobbles with light. Every cry ascending
reminds me now that the worst will happen,
has happened.
It's happening before I got here.

Le Maudit Maudit
Arthur Rimbaud

Even I, it's hysterical, have to keep coming back
to the campfire. There is no corner of the dark
unmollified by its gems, unedified by its wink:
the elf in the garden; shire where the kettle hissed
to the gas-light and mother muttered to father.

Even I, who'd forgotten ever having poked my snout
in the hen's bordello, or listened in the barn
to rain on the barn-roof; supra-prophetic timbre
of grain-sack and wood-stack; couldn't resist forever
the plush of kind: sweet gravity of the intimate spaces.

Even poetry has its comforts: the erotic
pageant created turbulence in the high chamber;
its degradations flickered all night on the mairie,
and grocers stumbled over their knobbed canes
when bangers went off like gunshots.

from Variations
Anselm Kiefer

3.
You turned away from the forest
which baffled you, but whose beasts were real.
You were never the one with the adze, but the attic
admits you anyway: its neat rows
of assimilated pine-logs, its nude planks,

help you to pause, consider the giants
and the dybbuks. It may be you will light a flame
of rushes dipped in resin from still-drooling boards:
twelve flames at equal intervals. This is panning out well:
you can come again when you need to, or never come again.

There is nothing sacred about it, there are only the flames,
which are not sacred at all, but recall
to the ordered woodpile, the assimilated forest,
what is forever dangerous in wood, brothered to you
by a kind of magic, a goety in the grain.

Domestic
Igor Stravinsky

Putting my hat aside for a moment;
putting aside my cane, my carte-de-séjour,
my buttonhole, my phylactery; putting aside my ring
engraved with the crest of the harlequin; my politesse;
my deeply ingrained sense of duty, fair-play, hospitality;

I swung the axe on the guest and the guest went down
like a sack of logs. I swung it, the axe bit
and the guest went down and stayed down: the illustrious guest,
the statesman, the one with his finger on the pulse.
The one with his fist on the pulse.

After that I forgot I was ever going out,
and started in on the furniture. It was possible to construct
from what was left, and even as the pieces flew,
a guest more pliable, less "true"; who could rig a deck
if he had to, but who never declared war on anyone.

The Space of Saying
Maurice Blanchot

We are not talking here about the blind men staggering
across a landscape entirely foreign to them:
one falls, the other falls, and where were they going anyway,
the beggars, the tramps, the scarecrows? We are talking about
an orderly procession of well-appointed denizens,

that might be a dance of sorts, or will possibly become one
when the eye closes on it and the scent of trauma
is carried away by the cooking smells when the lid comes off
the pot. For now, though, for now, whenever that is,
the leader must follow the others down the path marked
                                        out for them,

and move when they move, and hurry when push comes to shove,
and try to go straight ahead when the panic takes him;
and never, but never, never ever to turn his head
to the one who follows him, drags at him, the imminence
                                        that grips his ribs
in the half-light, the one he is effortlessly gaining upon.

The Banner
Akira Kurosawa

Of the several colours, the myriad tints;
of the hints, the nuances of the myriad avatars
of the one colour – shade, tone, voice –
occurring naturally or otherwise (sky notes,
earth, water notes, fire glints); it's up to you

to choose the ones already chosen for you –
to take them to heart and run with them. To choose
the forms, too: the configurations of belligerent metal,
already chosen for you, for you of all people
fortunate or otherwise; the music that they unfurl;

the war-place; the path to the citadel; tomb;
relations; counsellors; and be ready at once to hurl,
wherever the colours waver, at any given point,
wherever the colours fade and the different colours
fume in the leaves, that incredible crimson shout.

The Just
Henry Fonda

You were normal and it hurt us
to see the way they treated you,
because we knew they would treat us the same:
our heads would spout, ring out, in chiaroscuro
ditches; the bars would clang on our primal pain.

You kept your head up, though your shoulders sagged
perceptibly under the weight of the coming
outrage. You were ordinary, god help you,
but marked: you couldn't quite fit your limbs
to the shadow under the buzzard's wings.

You had to go through it all from the start,
and come out ready to begin.
That was your genius, though: to learn something,
and bring it home to dinner in the evening –
meat-loaf and homilies with the wife and kids.

Pilgrim
Geoffrey Chaucer

1.
I was there, I travelled with them
into the flatlands, keeping to the path
for fear of marshes. Some of them ran ahead,
and some ran off at a tangent. It was my job
to call the fool a fool and the wise man lucky

for travelling further than the ground they'd stood on.
At night you could hear the chants, see the incense
curdling amongst the rafters of the inns;
that oriel blush on the hams. When they broached the stories,
some of them were told by their stories. Well, I avoided them.

We found we were getting nowhere, were going
nowhere. The place was cavernous and ill-lit.
Words swarmed in the niches, straw poked, an occasional spark
flew out from its housing. It was my job
to laugh at the funny bits and to tend the horses.

2.
Some days I laughed so much
the horses broke their hobbles and ran off
through the reeds and were never seen again,
though some were ridden by the homing-flea
and clattered back rejoicing the way we came.

The world was cavernous, ill-lit and resembled an inn,
which, after all, is precisely what it was,
until the stories – then the gold peeped out
from the optic, a man's arm writhed like wood,
like vines, in erratic burgeonings. Then we were well away;

then we were ready for the journey of all journeys.
I couldn't tell you if we ever arrived,
or got any further than that worm-wracked table.
All of that is irrelevant anyway
when evenings fall, when destinies sink by the wayside.

Graham Hartill

Ghost Dance

the Earth is yellow
the Earth is blue
listen to this rhyme
grandfather
in your scorching nail factory, 1924
listen to my song
grandmother
stringing up rabbit-meat in your grocery shop
doing your accounts

the Earth is brown and wet
there is rain pouring on gaslit streets
take account of this song grandmother
it is pouring with rain

the Earth is white
the Earth is red
the bird may be dead
but the feather is still flying
the whirlwind blew
and your faces became water
the sun still shines on that running water
I can hear you
walking between the stars
I can hear you
patrolling up and down through time
this is
      the Ghost Dance

    *

– wild stars,
the faces before me.
My father's, strong,
exhausted,
30 years putting doors on cars,
two weeks day-shift,
two weeks night shift,
asks me if I've got a bob or two
and I say yes and he says
you're alright then?
Bear-man, looking after stomachs.

And my mother's, 72
still going strong,
looking after brothers, sisters
through the 30's and the War
with grandad out of work,
her angular, dark and respectable
face in a photo in the dining room,
and later, straight after marriage,
her wartime face.

*

the field is yellow
the field is red
listen to the snow
grandchildren
and to the heat
the field is brown and wet
there is wind in the streets

the sky is green
grandchildren
the sky is white
I wonder where you live?
the ground reclaims its own life

*

this is
            the Ghost Dance
the breadword
the colourword
eyes
my testicles

this city is our fathers
mothers
daughters
sons
or our faces be turned to the wall

the city of wind
the city of travellers

the city of day
the city of grass

            *

Fever Wind

This wind blow hot
        mother, father
this wind blow cold

        so cold it will freeze you

freeze your nerves
        so you'll never grow old
freeze your heart
        so you'll never feel cold

            fever wind singing: sunshine and moonshine
                dry out your bones

this wind blow cold
    brother, sister
wind blow hot

    so hot it will burn you

burn your nostrils
    so you can't smell burning
burn your heart
    so you can't feel a thing

    this fever-wind singing brother, sister
     fever wind singing sunshine and moonshine
    dry off your hands

     *

    fever-wind
     is a house on fire
    fever-wind
     is a ten-ton truck
    fever-wind
     a compulsive liar
    fever-wind
     is your good luck

fever-wind
  is a god in the tree-tops
fever-wind
  is a prisoner on the run
fever-wind
  is a word in your ear
fever-wind
  some guy with a gun

    fever-wind talks
     and you can't quite catch it

fever-wind laughs
    and you don't know why
fever-wind turns up
    when you least expect it
fever-wind opposite
    catching your eye

*

people will pay good money for a taste of the wind
it brings pictures loaded with savage flowers
a cargo of animals
and talking birds

    when the fever-wind blows
people collect together
    and try to catch it from each others' mouths

we will pay good money
    for a dose of it
for a blast of
the fever-wind

    the men wear their brightest dresses
        they look like flowers
        the women talk like animals
    the wind blows in and out of their mouths

our tongues become wild
        blue
                        birds
when it blows
    trees
        grow in our teeth
        songs
                        yellow and red
through the windows
    of broken houses

from Silver John

*"When evening shadows lengthen, it is not difficult to
believe that the reedy little tarn of Llyn Hilyn, near New
Radnor, is haunted by the spirit of a murdered man whose
body was thrown into it. The murdered man was known
as Silver John because of the silver buttons he wore upon
his coat. By some he is said to have been a cattle drover,
by others a skilful bone-setter and charmer, especially
expert in curing sick animals. . ."*

*

1. A Dream Song of Silver John

I'll crack your joints stretched backward on a hay-bale,
then kick you good up the arse.
What's up?
                I'll yank your neck like a goose.
What ails you,
                that a kick in the balls won't cure?
Crack your arm across your back
and haul you up like a bag of grass.
I'll double you up like a mouldy carpet from out of some
                                old woman's kitchen.
I'll pull your spine so fast and straight you'll shoot all over
                                the straw.
You'll yelp like a cock taking fright at a fox
it'll curdle the milk in the goat
and back'll pull out straight and your knuckles go off like
                                a gun.
I'll kick your bladder around all over the barn,
and pummel your guts like a red-faced wife at the doughboard.
I'll claw them out and wrap them round your neck and
                                pull them tight till -

I'll tear your wick off and feed it to frisky hens.
I'll tug off your toenails and use them for fishhooks.
I'll rip out your glottis and stick it in mine and sing your songs

then I'll go to your mucky house and I'll murmur your
                                             own sweet things
to your daughter and wife and son.
Your tongue'll make a supper cheap for your fat blue cat.
I'll suck out your eyes then stick them back the wrong
                                             way round,

    so when I'm done you won't know whether you're
                                             coming or gone -

               *

3. His Sickness

Catch your own reflection in his buttons,
His 30x30 pieces.
Silver John's no saint,
    no healer,
    poet,
    priest.
Is not a man.

Silver John's mother put cakes all over your body,
    then chewed them, one by one,
her sin-eating song in her nose, full seemly.

He doesn't inhabit a house,
    or flat,
    or tent,
    or van.
He doesn't live nowhere.

John absorbs your illness.
You name it:
    gut-rot, mad cow, second childhood.
Viruses beg him to let them come to him.

He prays for them to infect his songs
    so that no-one can understand him.

He makes up stories about his granny's drum,
his Japanese sister,
    the moon he embraced.
His tongue is as hot as a horseradish.

No Jobseekers' Allowance
    SS snoops,
    nor Neighbourhood Watch for John.
No Boots the Chemist or Marks & Sparks or Currys
                                frozen doorways.
Just an ague, and a walk, a walk, a walk.

Don't fret,
he won't tell anyone about
    your itch,
    your dizziness,
    your vacancy.
You're safe with him.

This money he wears,
    is a thousand mirrors
and after all,
    your offerings.

            *

Lay hair clips then,
    and broken bits of mirror,
    corners of postcards,
    little plastic bulls,
    and smeared algae jamjars
down at his well, his watering hole.

Listen hard to the woodpecker,
learn his rattle.
And then to the tick of the wood beetle.

Welcome the moth to your thumb,
and the bat to your bedroom.

Stick your head in the fox's den
put Golden Syrup out for badgers.

Paint your breast with wasps.
Look after nature's people.

*

5. Walking Towards His Death

Tonight my body's a tower of silence.
I'll die next Tuesday at half-past ten
not from cyanide or powdered granite
but tossed in a pond like a shit-tailed kitten
an insignificant village.

Out beyond the coast there was a country,
ancient roads lead nowhere to it.
A thousand died at Cantre'r Gwaelod,
the night Seithenyn, the floodgate guard,
got smashed on apple wine.
    Now axe-welts shimmer in lapping water,
clumps of hawthorn, willow, fir,
and teacups drip from fisherman's hooks.

Out beyond the coast of what we know,
there's still a body,
places that recur.
Tuesday, I'll gulp down
pulverised diamonds,
and leap at the edge of your mind for good,
    a slapping silver fish.

Chris Torrance

The Least Likely Buddha
(After Kerouac: I am the Buddha called The Quitter)

full moon madness badness frus-
tration grumble paranoia
                              I am not
that Buddha called The Quitter
I am the Least Likely Buddha

I am 3 rotties on one leash
I am a snaketooth corgi on an estate
I am a murder of crows pecking eyes out

I am a 70 ton bulldozer
razing an ecosystem
I am a necklace of traffic cones
strangling the articulate motorist

I am the Buddha
who will not be told
I am the fox
uneasy in the fold

I am the Buddha
not found in gold
I am the Buddha
you cannot behold

I am a jagged can bringing tetanus
I am a government
brought down in orgasms of prurience

I am the Buddha who left the Way
I am the Buddha on the twisting track
I am the Buddha who loves to stray
who wont walk the same way twice

I am the no-name Buddha
tracer of many paths, the road,
stately avenues, poachers creeps,
game runnels, badger boltholes

I am bloody violence
spewing out of hellfire
I am prime chaos poised
pendulum of eternity

I am a butterfly wing
                        I am
the Least Likely Buddha

The Slim Book
(two extracts)

snow-
grains
        & collies

run their muzzles
along the surface
with every appearance
of delight

                further down
the valley
is so vulgar
as to have
no snow

               this area
which stays nameless & remote
               blanket
afforested & distant

split by ravines, the valley floors
undrained   cultivation, if any
on favoured alluvial strips.
                    later,
at Ystradvellte, a
nucleated settlement

wicker wattles
daubed with mud
but dangerous, wolf & wild pig,
                    bears & bandits

hiding its seams of black wealth
                    under glacial till

when poetry
was news

when a poet
stood at the side
of every king . . .

               or I as
          unofficial bard to
               Brychan
          tripping him gently
          through drowsy firelight mead

a saint
for every day

& a song or a tale
for each & every one
of the 365 days
-the calendar memory
of the year*

*" . . . plainly those 365 bardic metres
were each day's measure of itself . . ."
-Robert Kelly, 'Alchemical Journal'

bottle, bake &
brew, hew &
cut to warm
& hoe again

thoth, the artificer,
the totter, the
cons-tit-tut-ion
                    hill

cobbled
street
straight up
to the sky
do you know
who you
really are?

I tranform
food to dung
dung to
compost

compost to
broad beans
& change
every cell

in my body
every 7
years

the experiments
of the alchemists
often met with
failure

seeking to transmute
"base metal to gold"

seeking to transmute
not gold but
self

even
fitted a
new element
to the

baby belling
cooker

without
being
cooked, without
being

"a properly qualified
person"

*

the nature of word

the nature of logos

changing every second

no, logic
must let it go
into flight

across synapse pulse, neuron
bolt, molecular frenzy,
gobbling negative speed-hole

time is a magma
erupting
to the surface of the lyric

Angel Busted

(for Chris Jenkins)

Mountains, moors, crags & quarryings,
rail inclines to the sky & beyond
estates on rolling hillspurs
unloved, tattered streets
torn posters ripping off
boarded shopfronts,
pale windy sunshine

flaring across silver rooves
to dunes & seas & drowned cities

privet shivers in a thrash of wind
leaves falling, words twisting
fierce twigs from the sun
caught in his sox
angel arrest rivets the coaltown
angel fries in cold steel
A sudden phalanx of paranoid swords
strident star sirens of interference
aluminium boneheads bleached of thought
hired guns, alloymen, disposal experts
crystalmen & dropmen, bagmen & dead bodies
tarnished warriors clanking their lasers masers
particle beam accellerators
cryptic fundamentalist mullahs arousing
from cold minarets

mirrorbright caffeine raps an easy smile
fierce twigs from the sun caught in his sox
angel arrest rivets the coaltown
angel fries in cold steel

privet shivers in a thrash of wind
hired guns, alloymen, disposal experts
crystalmen & dropmen, bagmen & dead bodies
posters ripping off rotted shopfronts

torn, unloved, tattered streets
estates on rolling hillspurs
strident star sirens of interference
angel arrest rivets the coaltown
angel fries in cold steel
angel fries in cold steel

Cliff Forshaw

The Buddhas of Bamiyan

*In March 2001, the Taliban authorities destroyed two huge
ancient figures of the Buddha at Bamiyan, Afghanistan.*

> I met a traveller from an antique land
> Who said: 'Two vast and trunkless legs of stone
> Stand in the desert...' Shelley, *Ozymandias*.

Here's what remains: colossal holes in rock.
Not even legs. Each trunk's just that: hollow,
an opened, empty, god-sized box.

Raided tombs, recesses shaped like Pharaohs'
coffins or their huge cast shadows.
At their absent ancient feet: boulders,

rubble, mortar casings, spent ammo shells,
Taliban on Toyota trucks - *Allahu
Akbar!* ...Meanwhile, back in Kabul,

it's hush-hush Video Night - venue:
the old *World-Wide* language school. Banned,
but what the hell. Soldiers, perhaps ex-students,

scratch lengthening beards, bum smokes
or fiddle softpacks from black turbans.
Some place Kalashnikovs in stooks,

pass round a plastic lighter, trade contraband,
squat on the mat. Swarzenegger's back.
Tonight his sneer of cold command's

getting personal with a laser-sighted
45 slide; while the late-model terminator,
unperturbed, just mops up punishment,

absorbs whatever's handed out. Boof!
And - here's the groovy thing - from it he learns
to - how you say? - shape-shift, *morph*.

Once Buddha was just an empty throne.
Round here his face grew Greek or Persian,
half-way between Apollo and a king.

Xerxes, or Iskander perhaps, robes grown
stony with potency. Or Kanishka,
whose idea these statues were. - His own

headless statue stood back in Kabul:
enormous pantaloons, mighty kingly feet.
He got his last week. Full circle.

For centuries, huge mummies
wrapped in grubby bandages of rock
stood here, blind to passing armies.

Today, they blew away his legs and chin
- tank shells, rocket launchers - then
dynamited that big mother up to heaven.

It took twenty-five explosions
to wipe the smile right off that face,
incarnate him as dust, air, an empty throne.

Bars of light across eyes, mouths that whisper
through the hatches of shapeless prisons:
women, in *chador, burqas,* watch the distance,
rebel gunfire where the mountains rise.

The Poet's Stick

In Fort William museum there is a stick that belonged to Ian Lom, the Keppoch Bard, one of the greatest of the Gaelic poets. Supposedly, he lost his sword at the Battle of Inverlochy and used this stick to fight his way home. However, he did not fight in the battle as he had left his sword at home. He turned down the offer of a weapon from Alasdair mac Cholla Chiotaich, saying that he was required to celebrate the victory in song, and if he died there would be no one to praise the victors.

More enemies than
you could shake a stick at.
Gnarled, a lightning-blasted limb,
lignin gone arthritic.
The poisoned ink
of flytes and curses grown thick,
nib curdling, sprouting tic-quick
feathers: a quill-spill of crotch-itch, oxster-reek.
The slow creep of scabs,
a cloak of toad's skin
hiding the tongue's duplicitous iron,
its blade of shining insult scabbarded in an arse-lick.
The quintessence
of bile hardening each excrescence.

Weasel words in search of the perfect egg:
ferret backbone, stoat's
spine like a tongue licked over bark.
The cursed frog caught in the wooden throat.

Along the warp of wood,
useless whorls and nubs
where leprosy's put the idea of fist
into an open palm.

Ghost fingers beckon nowhere, the stubs
of blunted choice.

Twisted, an imp's knobkerry,
devil's knob, a warty
satanic woodie, shlong of shillelagh,
the ever-crowing cock.
No one's game bird. Flown. Woodcock.

Out of the hand and into the bush.
Could be the singer's
grave stave or God's
admonitory finger;
Aaron's miraculous almond-blossomed rod
or the diviner's compass twitching at springs
deep in the rock.

A spirit sword, a wand,
fit only for fighting hobgoblins, elves,
malignant lying shadow-selves,
guzzel-dogs and drunken puke-spattered gnomes,
whatever greasy inhabitants
of the turf between here and home.

In the real world it would crack
like tinder, or bend, sappy, snap back
a smart retort, this poet's lame excuse.

Shank's pony, is it?
The toe-stub heath rolling like a big sea.
A club-foot to stamp out hobbled trochees.
Paeans of praise
for all those who lie
like Lazaruses unraised.

Sea Changes

The odd warm winds keep up. The sea's
wrinkling with red weed. It weaves through the water
where slime hardens to stone. This jetty's
just frayed ropes and rotten planks, warty

with limpets now. Half sunk, a waterlogged
dory's choked up on a frayed tether.
The low sun turns distance to fogged
film, sky simmering. The weather's

so weird these past months. The sea
thickens nightly to a muscled slime, twitches
with the low flap of leather wings. At dawn, bees
swarm over drift-wood and drown. Smith's bitch

ate her litter. Nights I swat bugs, scan the heavens
for meanings. Old Ma Jones flicks cards. Paul
and the others drink. I'd leave, but Stevens
says there'll be work in the Fall.

I don't know why I feel so bruised.
Migratory birds flit like erratic needles.
Strange winds buffet their plumage.
They take off, and land again, confused.

Bar-Life

1. Girl

Doesn't see herself as a hooker, though there's a fine
to take her away before shift's over.
Has friends from far-off places: Yanks, Canucks,
Poms, Frogs, Krauts, Eyties.
Eyes herself in the mirrored backdrop,
looking good in red silk slashed mid-thigh,
swivelling her barstool between Madonna and the King,
She's lucky, not like the faded flowers,
the withered, the needle-ghosts,
the sick-chicks who work the show-bars
until their muscles get too slack.
Not like Bel, Meun, Noi, definitely not like Poni.

Some dead girl's kid sister goes the rounds
chaining jasmine over likenesses of H.R.H.
Serene, Most Very High, who wrote our anthem that is
                                        Falling Rain.
Maybe later English songs to which she has collected words,
odd ones stacked up on serviettes, ripped beer mats,
puzzles which don't quite work out right.
But now they play Girl Power very loud,
her head is a noisy crossword,
the Spirit House is jumping, partying with candles, caked
                                        with light.
But, in undusted corners, incense has already got tired:
perfumed ash coils, ghost-turds.
Next year she will have a baby, meet the right Farang
who will send her bucks and a ticket.
Next year, before she thickens further,
ends up like Sad Girl who didn't buy the bar.

But they have arrived, the boys in loud shirts:
hair slick from showers, neon-licked, newly-awake,
surprised to be found alive, here in Angel City.
She checks her lips, flicks a Marlboro from the soft-pack,
inserts it in the new cherry pout,
zeroes in on the one with kindest eyes,
feeling the pocket above his heart
for some kind of friendly fire.

2. Old Farang

Each year for winter, each year a little longer,
the company pension stretched as burning afternoons
dawdle through beer suds, the minutiae of *The Bangkok Post*.
Happy hour, chicks chilling out in the air-con;
street food, the humid intimacy of night. Show bars.
Wait till late, hit that special place when the girls are
                                        checking off.

Cheap rate till dawn, sometimes the weekend-wife.
Take her for a meal. One-sided conversation.
Short-time girls with short-term memory bad as his.
Long-time, he remembers only too well.

Pucker of stitches where her breasts had been as he bathed her;
kids who don't write anymore. No point in Christmas
                                        elsewhere.
And now death can take whatever toll it choose.
By the time it gets him, it'll be too late.
Can't be any other way. Already is way, way too late.

Mazatecan Witch

Huautla de Jímenez, Oaxaca, Mexico

You learned lore from soil, skins, stars,
stained yourself earth, interred yourself in sky.
Squatting out the rainy season,
high up, your mushrooms waited:
smoke snaking the belly of a cloud.
Your dog snarled through dank fugged leafage.
The wood was alive, whitened,
Sperm-spat with tiny cocked triggers.

For the men, life was down there:
cantinas, work, women, horses.
Mexico meant burnt water, eloquent liquors:
Mezcal, a stubborn ember under pissed-on ash;
Pulque, a green lily stinking of sweating meat.
But for you, Spanish was a gattling stuttering
somewhere off in sea-green jungles,
away below an armada of cloud.

An anthropologist took you away from yourself,
put you before lights, cameras, banal magic.
Your body swarmed to moths,
fame drawing each cell flameward,
then singed them back wingless. Flesh.

Your hair's cables frayed, twisted to ash,
as your old coiled power sprung,
slithering off through damp grass lushes
before electric twine whinnied the air.

The dull chink of coins sent you back,
to your earth-box cabin,
to mend the mesh where jackals had smirked through,
got at your chickens; the wet pelt of mist
nuzzling you like a stray dog come home.

Sitting among the arthritic ruins of your domain,
you wear your century of years
like the knuckles of a bone necklace,
Below your hut, the Municipalidad challenges
your claim of sky with a white-walled clinic.

Your cracked voice is now reserved
for coughing out songs onto tape.
A corpse's great granddaughter is your daily tongue:
ancient silences interpreted through Rosita's giggling Spanish,
bargaining out your mysteries.

Every week they come, no matter the season,
with shiny spectacles, good boots,
big nosy cameras, folding money,
for dried curls of skin in creased brown paper,
salamanders blackening in old jars of crystalized honey.

Beyond the new coffee fields, thinking of plundered power,
your eye seeks out new secret silos.
You catch a scent that somehow reminds you
of the runt you trained to nose out where
power was just about to finger through.

Pascale Petit

The Strait-Jackets

I lay the suitcase on Father's bed
and unzip it slowly, gently.
Inside, packed in cloth strait-jackets
lie forty live hummingbirds
tied down in rows, each tiny head
cushioned on a swaddled body.
I feed them from a flask of sugar water,
inserting every bill into the pipette,
then unwind their bindings
so Father can see their changing colours
as they dart around his room.
They hover inches from his face
as if he's a flower, their humming
just audible above the oxygen recycler.
For the first time since I've arrived
he's breathing easily, the cannula
attached to his nostrils almost slips out.
I don't know how long we sit there
but when I next glance at his face
he's asleep, lights from their feathers
still playing on his eyelids and cheeks.
It takes me hours to catch them all
and wrap them in their strait-jackets.
I work quietly, he's in such
a deep sleep he doesn't wake once.

My Mother's Clothes

The air was full of Gitane Filtre, her reflection

transformed by the spray that lifts from torrents,
the wardrobe door open, her clothes pristine.

Some were in polythene, preserved in the mist
from the day they were worn; a blue and peach suit

striped with Iceland's primeval landscape
where fire and ice hiss under Northern Lights.

She told me about her year in the Indian Embassy,
unwrapped a sari deep as the Gokak Falls,

charged with rust-red debris. Its many mirrors
retained faces of her admirers.

Right at the back, trailing along the wardrobe floor,
her bridal-dress was a river shot with scales of salmon.

Next were négligés, subterranean springs
cascading down slopes of mountains,

then a dressing-gown which towered in the frosty depths,
its cataract of ice fastening at her throat;

an emerald trouser-suit with matching silk blouse
was a secret chute from the South of France

where she'd tried to make us a home.
I fondled the ruff, its underwood trickle.

After that, there were no more choice materials,
only dull tweeds, sober crêpes for the mature woman,

modest falls in the Welsh hills where she'd settled.

Self-Portrait with Fire Ants

To visit you Father, I wear a mask of fire ants.
When I sit waiting for you to explain

why you abandoned me when I was eight
they file in, their red bodies

massing around my eyes, stinging my pupils white
until I'm blind. Then they attack my mouth.

I try to lick them but they climb down my gullet
until an entire swarm stings my stomach,

while you must become a giant anteater,
push your long sticky tongue down my throat,

as you once did to my baby brother,
French-kissing him while he pretended to sleep.

I can't remember what you did to me, but the ants know.

The Ant Glove

Dear Father, after Mother's death, after I'd read
    all your letters to her and her letters to you

and finally understood that I was the fruit of her rape,
    I walked into the forest.

The tribe I met there helped me write this letter
    preparing me as they would prepare a boy

who wanted to become a man.
    The elders raided nests of giant hunting ants

for three hundred shining black workers
    which they wove into the palm fibres of a glove,

their stinging abdomens pointing inwards.
    They blew on them to enrage them.

They painted my writing hand with black dye
    from the genipap fruit and thrust it into the glove.

I had to remain silent while the ants attacked.
    Can you smell the lemony scent of formic acid?

These words are dancing the Tocandeiro.
    I hope you're dancing as you hold my letter,

as I had to dance wearing the ant glove
    stomping my soles hard on the ground.

Afterwards I cut the stones from my feet.
    Afterwards I celebrated with a feast

biting off ant-heads to suck blood from their bodies
    until my lips and tongue were numb.

I hope you've sucked the blood from the words
    that stung you. My hand is still swollen.

Are your fingers swelling as they stroke my signature?
    Are your lips and tongue numb from kissing my kisses?

My hand is always in the glove, writing goodbye,
    red and blue feathers flutter from my wrist.

The Mineral Mother

Your face has the violet luminescence
of the long dead.
Night after night I dreamt of this descent
until I reached the basalt door
where you wait to greet me,
your irises streaked like falcon's eye gems.
You lead me into the crystal crypts
that form in magma over time,
down smoky quartz rooms
where you live now,
your rock crystal skull
shot with tourmaline needles.
Your veins are fire opal.
I have come with my hammer and chisel
to break you up into jewels
that I can bring back to the surface.

Skins

I am sewing the skins of birds end to end.
Snakeskins, woodskins, even the skin on water
must be dried, conserved, worn.
I am wearing my grandmother's spirits.
Her skin was rough from too much work –
I flay a tree, proof the bark for the river.
Her skin was soft from too much rain
but I cannot wear water.
So I have come to the world's loudest storm
to hear her sing. The sky-skin rips.
Her cheeks appear, wrinkled with lightning.

Embrace of the Electric Eel

For thirty-five years, Father, you were a numb-fish,
I couldn't quite remember what it felt like

that last time you hugged me when I was eight,
just before you went away.

But when you summon me to your stagnant pool,
Dad, Papa, whatever I should call the creature

that you are, now you finally ask for my love:
do you think I've become strong as the horses

Humboldt forced into a stream
to test the voltage of Amazonian eels?

He had never witnessed
"such a picturesque spectacle of nature"

as those great eels clamped against the bellies
of his threshing horses, how their eyes

almost popped out and their manes stood on end.
Though the jolt alone did not kill them,

many were so stunned they drowned.
That's how it is, Father, when you open your arms

and press your entire length against my trunk.

Portrait of My Mother as Xipe Totec

When she said she was Xipe Totec
Aztec god of springtime, I believed her.
Sitting me down opposite her rocking-chair
she explained what that meant:
she needed to flay my skin
and dance in it in the sunshine.
We had no net curtains then,
the neighbours always looked in
when she turned on the lights.
There was no TV, just her face
which shone like a screen
I couldn't help watching
but wished would break down.
I wondered whether the people passing
saw how she entered me, and if
I would ever stop shivering
as if I'd been skinned. My hands
hung from her wrists like mittens.
My tongue, behind her lips,
asked her how she was feeling.
"Better" she smiled, "now that the seeds
are sprouting in the fields."
She walked out of the front door.
And I found myself dancing alone on the lawn –
a hollow sheath, golden, shot with green.

Self-Portrait as a Yanomami Daughter

I've built a rainforest shelter,

painted *hekura* on the walls –
my only visitors, these helper-spirits.

I haven't been out since you died.
Like a good Yanomami daughter

I've kept our fire alight.
Your body made it burn so fiercely.

My hair singed as I raked
the embers for all your bones

to grind to a black powder.
When I finished, the *hekura* spoke.

They told me to shave my hair
and braid it into a belt,

bind it tight around my waist
the way you used to hold me, Father,

when you turned into a demon
and tore me with your penis.

This is how Night was made,
my thighs sticky with star-blood,

my mouth flooded with moonseeds.
Now, I wear a child's necklace

threaded with toucan beaks.
I shake my rattle,

stamp my clapping stick.
I pour your ashes into plantain soup.

The first sip makes me retch,
then I learn to like the taste.

Portrait of My Brother as an Endurance Runner

Now that I know the secrets
of the Tarahumara tribe
famous for their long-distance races,
I urge my brother not to eat
Mother's fatty meals. Instead
I feed him rabbits, deer, rats.
Then mix the blood of a turtle
with the blood of a bat
and roll it with tobacco
into a cigar for him to smoke.
I dress him in loose clothes,
dry the head of an eagle
for a charm around his neck,
hang deer-hoof rattles from his waist.
Before Mother stirs, he sets out
at a steady pace, not fast
at first, but never slowing,
until he's run forty miles
in six hours. And so he continues,
the rattlers keep him awake.
Strips of mountain lion skin
protect his ankles.
When night falls, torches
of resinous pinewood are lit
and held by strangers
along the steep forest path.
He keeps on running until
he's old enough to realise
it's better to live in a cave
up a deep canyon alone
than to stay in his mother's house.

The Flying Bed
after Frida Kahlo

After the third miscarriage
what else could I do
but erect the bed-easel
and paint so furiously

my bed levitated
　　　out of the Henry Ford hospital

into the region of giant hailstones
where my baby girl
floated in her altocirrus dress.

While the nopal cactus
opened its blood-red blossoms on my sheet
I painted an eagle
with its wings on fire.

I looked down at the Rouge River complex
and every factory hissed
like the steam sterilizer

everything moved like a landsnail.

I raised the mirror
and began my self-portrait.

The Bald One gave me a necklace
of desert dew.

She called me Xochitl –
　　　　Flower of Life,
　　　　　　Pantocrator.

I flashed her a smile – my teeth
capped with rose diamonds.

Remembrance of an Open Wound

after Frida Kahlo

Whenever we make love, you say
it's like making love to a crash –
I bring the bus with me into the bedroom.
There's a lull, like before the fire brigade
arrives, flames licking the soles
of our feet. Neither of us knows
when the petrol tank will explode.
You say I've decorated my house
to recreate the accident –
my skeleton wired with fireworks,
my menagerie flinging air about.
You look at me in my gold underwear –
a crone of sixteen, who lost
her virginity to a lightning bolt.
It's time to pull the handrail out.
I didn't expect love to feel like this –
you holding me down with your knee,
wrenching the steel rod from my charred body
quickly, kindly, setting me free.

PC Evans

The Definitive Farewell

The laughing room
Is filled with lost life
Music springs sprinkling
Through doors and windows
Some dead black singer
Crying off the blue walls
Between the posters
Intimately touches
The battle-scarred
Dining.
Nicola is preparing salad
In the restaurant kitchen
I preserve a distant sense of intimacy
A closing sense of urgency.
Raging, dispossessed
On the telephone
To thou
My bored confessor
Hunted rabbit-eyes caught in the glare
Of self-explanation
Too much too ridiculous anger
Entertaining the mealed.
Lying naked in a tiny attic
Wind on the tiles on the roof
To be whispered to
In the darkness
Three times
I love you
And respond believing everything
While the sun is selling pizza
At a nearby location.
A little German hexagram

In purple and blue starred leggings
Roller-skating through Zurich
With a Venezuelan transvestite
On shopping night
Love's nature illuminates
And merchandises
As the morning rises
Like a swamp mist
On this red light street
And Orpheus limps home
Tendons slit
Past the windows
To a coffin
Half-built.

A Short History of Lust

> ...esse delendam.

Mithras had forbidden unto Mani the dewy grape,
even Augustinus, with Hippo, defended the law –
The buttocked peach was only for the gods to take,
and the asparagus, dear ladies, ask of it no more...

Fellatio and Cunnilingus, clowns from Ostia, south of Rome,
went roving merry the flat globe round,
Cunnilingus with a peach, and the good Fellatio
with a creamy asparagus in his painted mouth -

Hippo went to ruin on the old Carthaginian shore,
for an old Carthaginian shore is the best,
like Tanit and Dido. And lastly, to rest,
there's been nothing since then but lust and more
lust and luxuria, three gilded ells high. And Vi
behind a window, humming as her money multiplies -

After Hans R. Vlek

Prayer For Abercynon

Running the field of fern
Where there are no paths
Ferns high above the head
Running blind
Skipping tussock and rock
Like a deer
Racing headlong
Down the mountainside
And coming up
Where grass resumes
Breathless above
A dry-stone wall

And years later, as adolescents, climbing
Back up to First Peak
From where you can see
Down the valley
How the river disappears
Past the small round rocks
That found a beach of cobbles
In the hook of the river
Under the eyes of the coal tips
That focus to the sea
The shaft of the glimmering river
Drawn from the quiver
Of Cardiff Bay
And fired away

I thought only of land without demarcation
No system of ownership and fences
Far from the ribbons of patchwork terraces
That so shame the valley
I could hardly admit
That I belonged to it

But now with Holland like a chain around my neck
That lush land too
Rank for the seed
With its vertiginous need
For comfort and certainty

I look back to the country
Where atrophy stares from the face of every man
Their lives on the torn streets
Of grey stone and slate
Amongst dilapidated churches, pubs and Workman's halls
Are lit only by the reflection
Of their technological
Recreation

And though each generation
Dies back
As waste flesh
Into the dark ground
Where the seeds scatter
Or the new shoots wither
It is for want of belief only
Belief like water falling
On the sleeping ground
Water untainted by the lies
Of the coin and the cross
And the sense of failure

And though the winds blow vile on the mountainsides
And on the houses below
Where the villagers shelter
Let their lives flame
With a simple pride
That the river may once again
Bring life
For this is not dead ground
This is fallow ground

Rest Bay

Soft, soft night
Fog over the water
The moisture on my beard
Looking over the Amstel
To the fog-softened lights
Of the island.

There is one point
On the Welsh coast
Where a line can be drawn
Without interruption
To the coast of Peru.
My father told me this.

I have been drinking red wine
I feel something is coming
To an end
I have a reluctance to depart
Staying brings nothing new,
Brings nothing
Life is unfolding
I have a dull nostalgic envy.

Ezra Pound 1943

For Tyrolean absolution
He wanders,
Not abashed,
Perhaps no longer confused.

Blistered feet soaking in
The cool waters
Of Lake Garda;
Hacking wood like a frontiersman.

The poet behind the painter's
Beard,
Beneath the composer's red
Hair,
With wit and manners
Charms his captors
And prepares for home.

'It is the quality of the affection -
- In the end -
That has carved the trace in the mind.'

Dove sta memoria?
What cold beauty
Separates the man
From life?

*

I don't know your house
I thought perhaps I'd go there
Does it lie between forest and mountain?
Your voice on the telephone distantly echoes

Do you still play to relax
That old skin drum?
Your hands are so awkward and heavy
You're just as masculine as I
It's a wonder we ever made love

Do you remember the night
We camped by the lake?
When all the wild rabbits were dying
Slow in the light on the side of the water
And the dog trying to run them down

A Flight of Gulls

The river nestles the crane
And the flag
And the iron red hut
In the curve of its arm;
The loaded barge snowploughs the water,
Gravelled to the water-line.

The heron's grey gaze
On the river
Bank, and the quill
By the ferry shore,
Are incongruous in this brief confluence
Of light, unquestioning, sky.

Suddenly seagulls break
To tack to
A colloquy of marketeers
And aged traders,
The waters cracking with their cries as the gulls
Elide their river to the rich tide.

Then the driving of piles continues
And we fly
Away from the river
With a burning cry,
As though the river was touched by the fists of the sun,
Not the hands of a greedy Dutch town.

When evening comes it is winter.
A newspaper
Arcs in the wind
And declines; the hands
Of the railway are reeling in the distance like a debt;
And the city respires in a halo of its breath.

I hear only the sound of a train.

*

I do not have to catch each falling leaf
It's enough to know the leaves are falling

*

When we were tired
Our love making
Was tired
When we were angry
It was angry
Every period has its own art

*

A pumpkin head
With a gash of teeth
In a slit of mouth
Hewn from pulp
And no candle lit
And if there was
Blown out

Patrick Jones

autumn eternal

in rainleafed pouringpuritythisdrazzzling waterseems to
closecomfort
seemstosafeusinandallow peace somehow
how the slippingsound pourssafetyandneedfornothingbut
shelter
so
how one must constantly reassess, pull the blinds down
for days, hide, question, find the core of oneself like
this sundaying rain,
it seems to say,
stay,
for there is much to be done,
stay
for sanctity is your soul
stir in your stay
stay,
and for your mind to be whole
remainlikethissoakedbrownearththatsurrounds
accept the rain
the mist morning and blackchlorophyll night
accept and be free,
deny and lay chained to narcissism forever –
allowance of the cold
will eventually warm
be little in your days
and huge in eternity
fill cracks mend tears
pour language into fears
speak

of
silence sadness soul
and somehow   some place
you will be you
like this rain
this simplicity of speech
be
and all shall be along with you
biblebled days of sundayed rain across these vortexed
valleys
see how the factories close
the names change but the exploitation doesn't
see how they run
when the rain rizzles down
but the mountains
stand like silent fathers
watching   seeing   being
holding our skin to a semblance of saturation
dreamed of
a natural emancipation
rejoice in this rain
redream your dreams
be near to your thoughts
cut your cuts
and wound your wounds
and form a cuticle to regret
and
let
the rain
thread through your arteries
to the unknown territories
you know so well –

infusion

simplicity is the bounty of breath
and in this petrification
an emancipation
shadows stutter our sun
mindosuction melts our memories
until balance breaches and beginnings end
yet still shelter is inherent in everything we crave
creation is a metaphysical act
untamed unfettered by what should be
yet still   still yet
our lives, placenta
our thoughts, sustenance
our acts, beautiful
our questions, answers
our existing, enough
and as your body fills with another
so do i and the future glitters as glazed fingernails
and i think of you growing and glowing
frightening yet inspiring
poignant but everlasting
a star shone silence in a satellite sky
as i a slow leaf clinging to bark
let go,
fearing the fall
yet needing the wind.

reach

and nothing is perfection
holes
fill
everything
hands fasten in mind distance;

aloneness the companion we cling to
when flesh fails.
if only
only if
repeat
recite
dissonance
of a world unfit for this living.
how
do we signify
what makes contact mean
if and wish constantly recoil into how;
and i cannot find the place for it.
the
violation
of the one
is the isolation of the two
yet the clock stutters sadness
and time oceans along
indifferent to the apostate of hearts
that once bled together
now stab each other
so
nail hope to the bandage
crush fracture into flowers

can.
can
belonging
ever
belong

again?

christmas lights in january

rain beat my soul
empty me in
drizzling distances heart sedated
isolations
isolate
and dignify
us
tears
come to signify

a defiance
a shroud
a loss
a dolphinned silence
of uninterrupted eloquence.

strung out like eyes
cold as worship
bleeding blood colour over sun denied streets
they
watch
they
wait
like Jesus upon Calvary

to be
dragged down
and put away
until
until

another
sense
of
belonging

occurs.

fathers' day 2000

today,
i walk head down neck beat mindworn shouldnersnapped against
the vitriolic afterburn of unman
today
i do not know how to hold my head up for my gender
stare ahead – too cold
stare away – coward
cry   too feminine
hold back   egotistical

picture me in a frame
carbon me into you
xeroxed testosterone throated in derelict muscles
hold me in my history
pour me another malt whiskey
castrate me for the present
denote me my future.as
the femination of my realization
is my downfall
the prozacpulse of necrophiliac emancipation
to be
to be
to be

a
man
this man
now
today
who shakes inside at the soiled portrait that stares from
celluloid

that spits from terraces
that imprisons feelings
that is afraid to be afraid
that is
i
only know
that it is easy
to become a father
but
so much
harder
to be one;

Samantha Wynne-Rhydderch

First Aid Class

I kneel there with the head gardener in my arms,
feeling the pulse in his neck the way he touches
leaves in real life, his skin a series of impressions
on calico beside me. Everyone an iridologist
dressing head wounds with the enthusiasm
of the starched in field hospitals before 1915.

We learn that fainting is merely the rearrangement
of blood, my bronchial tree simply a cameo of me,
but more vitriolic. I am eager to see the cyanosed
around the edges, intuit a cardiac arrest.
Now and then I hear the thrum of a defibrillator,
arterial gestures from the past. Handling a rib-cage
over lunch I have a sense of ornament.
Finally we study a handout of unconsciousness,
poison ivy groping at the window panes.

I imagine us meeting under other circumstances,
coy about our intimacy. Then I begin to understand
the way surgeons avoid the resuscitated
in *The Lamb & Flag*, the gardener playing cribbage
something too abstract, why terminology matters:
"terracotta" to "red", "episode" only a dot
on a screen.

We are asked to elevate a limb: the rituals of a sacrament,
the illustrations in the manual mute in savagery
as my hands around those open veins.

Willow Pattern

When you dropped the plate, the bridge broke
in two and the tiny blue ferns were torn.
Like us they would not mend. They spoke
in their dismembering; we could not mourn.
I wrote your name in willowy
handwriting on a scrap of paper, dropped
it in a jar of jasmine tea
which three hours in the freezer turned to rock.

On our first walk I plucked a fern,
arranged it in a cast full of hot wax.
Now the candle is almost burnt
away, a hard miniature pool acts
as evidence on a plate, a spell
cast and lost on a pagoda shell.

Père Lachaise

A tilting virgin offers me a snowball
as I pass, but I
could never accept such transience in the palm.
Her eyes are sealed with lichen,
her smile bites a century's feigned
indifference, and those cracked wings
ground her between inscriptions.

It's far, this sound of stone
that mitigates the frost.
A bare shroud holds us numb
and voiceless as Edith Piaf
locked up inside her porchway.
Reliquaries crowd us out.
Their letters bleed green.

The Hunt

I: The Hunt

A hound forever at her throat, the white hart
with her patterned antlers is caught again
and again on your wallpaper, the forest

intimate in the corners of your back room,
slightly furred as the dark underside
of leaves hidden by the sideboard. A falcon

stiff on his master's postured left arm, his men
red-braided in pursuit, each with a
bright spear raised. That winter you leapt like a stag

across the stream in Cwm Tudu, untextured,
broke a stalagtite and brought it back
intact for me, an elusive wand, with both hands.

II: The Engagement

Soon it will be fifteen years since the door closed
behind your musky shadow sliding
into that Tennysonian garden, August

on its breath, the evening waves' voltage in your voice
singing *Dafydd y Garreg Wen* out
to me, curled on the sea wall, my tailpiece wound

over the stones where you nightly held my bones
like china to your lips. Poacher, you
pledged always to unclip my magnolia hair

and let it flow over your shoulder's broad ledge
until that day when moonlight should fail
to slice Bala Lake in two, silver as my ring.

III: The Betrayal

I listened to the shell on your mantelpiece.
It sang to me of arms and men and
all that guff I've heard before. How many ears

cherished its lies? The seagull you told me you'd
shot over Cei Bach still falls screaming through
my head. I feel the wax on my feathers melt

as I plunge towards the headland castle
whose turret you spent hours re-pointing.
Stretching my arm across the bed will not warm

its marble. The wind howls back your name. Torn sails
flap on my line. In my dream I cut
your hair as you sleep: I've been sharpening my quill.

Report

Of how I slept with an open map by the bed
all night, tracing his past like a detective
in my dreams, inhaling placenames he'd mentioned
over a drink that evening, hoping they'd thrive
merely through sleep, seep into veins, these words.
Ancestry like geography is a blur, white
as a main road, blue as a moonlit cove.

Writing becomes a requirement, a dial
on the gauge of inevitability.

Each morning the ache unfurls, a refusal
to be rolled up in a winding-sheet, wholly
alive, elaborate as needlework, full
blooded as a matador intricately
trussed under the hot afternoon sun, ready.

Blackshaw Head in the Wind

They discuss land at the bar. I drain my glass.
Remnants of binliners screech in the trees
like crows. The houses are brutal by twilight,
the colour of the moon intravenous as your voice
on the mobile, adjectives flickering on the moors
like house lights in the valley below.

The greenery a brocade at the cemetery gate,
I am scoured down to bare quartz,
forced across the church wall. Wind traps my breath.
The gravestones rise like accusations I can't
answer. I've seen them leering at me
in nightmares – that begonia feeling.
I mean strictly ballroom, but galeforce.

Paramilitary Lover

He strokes my neck like the barrel of a rifle
he might have killed that German with,
his boots by the door, susceptible to the cold.
I glow by the fire in tandem with
the rosewood dresser, impartial to flames,
me with a passion for granite, him
with his head shaved against the night,
shedding his armour plate by plate.
I sleep under his shield, enfolded

in an English flag I think will
become my shroud. While I thrill
among the lilies, placing a chestnut
on the grate like a move in chess,
I see the incentive of lace
defeat artillery hands down.

The Café Excelsior, Montmartre

Their fingertips touch
under an Art Deco lamp
pouring honey onto his blurred lips.
She can't speak any more -
the Chablis has gone to her head.
Instead she peels the silk scarf
from his neck and strangles
it between anaemic fingers.
Her mahogany eyes are haloed
by chandeliers
which dazzle him. He can't stop
searching, scrutinizing
the negative of himself
in the Steinway, its lid an open coffin
breathing out magnetic notes
like Sirens that have plunged him
into his own whirlpool.
But you, you are embedded in me
like a rusty nail.

The Truth About Escalators

You can risk nothing with escalators.
They flow to the floor below,

their neat teeth pulling you down,
down. Rectangular waves

blend into an estuary of the bodiless
on rails. I feel myself hanging

among them while you go on
without me. Soon I will never see you

again: you will slip into a glass underworld
while I miss my step up here.

They are as beguiling as metronomes,
seeming to bring us closer as we move

further apart and each floor pours
us onto new levels of loss. Although

you are only one step away,
my personal space can never spill over

into yours: harmony is precisely
what keeps us apart.

There is no going back.
The escalator decides for us.

Rowndio'r Horn*

One by one they clipped the edge of the table
and smashed in the Lower Mess Deck, sixteen plates,
castanets. Candelabra you like, the sea
has reasons of its own. In the third watch she,
the mainsail, full-blown ivory, eighty-four
degrees to the wind, visceral to starboard
tore. Know her to be your shroud, think majestic
stone pier, tomb far from here, hers your cameric shirt.

Like everyone else in the Yacht Club, I pose
and tilt at Mar del Plata a hundred years
later, mermaid for the day, pina colada
in hand. Taffeta angle, sweet sail did you
call out to me, at the helm, as my feet flew,
caressed the deck, unintentional dancer?

---

*"Going round the Horn". Many New Quay sea captains sailed
round Cape Horn and returned to tell the tale. One who did
not was my great-great grandfather, Captain Edward Jones
('Tadcu Stryd Ganol') whose ship, *The Adventurer* was lost with
all hands (including his 19 year old nephew) on a voyage from
Taltal to Talcahuano off the coast of South America in March
1893. This sonnet was commissioned by the BBC for National
Poetry Day 2001.

Cecilia Rossi

Writing Stones

No – don't say you cannot write for lack
of paper, pen – not after she wrote
on a bar of soap with a hair pin,
or in the air, learning lines as prayers,
smuggling them into the world when she was
handed paper. They also wrote
on Rizla, folded words neatly as
sweets wrapped up in foil, then
swallowed them. Bowelled in
they made their way from prison
to prison, linking place, thought, hope.
A fair exchange: a poem for a smoke.
So, here: break this piece of slate,
grab this flat stone: write.

Now

They have more of us
than we do —
these local tourists from Bihar
taking snapshots of the white couple
on the beach, now the Monsoon
rains have ceased temporarily.

His blue eyes smile into the camera.
Her white skin gleams in the heat.

Even then our holidays smiled back at us
from the past.

Speaking in Tongues

He spoke the language of sand.
His rasping fricatives carved raw sounds
in the air between us; his sibilants slid
as though trapped inside an hourglass;
purple grains timed his voice as it
grazed the surface of my skin,
bedding against my skull like a thin
film of moss –

I answered in the language of water.
Let my vowels flow to fill the empty space
inside his plosives, claiming every corner
like the sea among rocks,
releasing his vibrant breath suddenly –
a magnolia of meaning,
a rare song in unison with the wind
and the moon.

The River's Trail

Once again the river
takes me on its trail.
The air is wet on my face.

A gravel path
where the undergrowth
gives way

to browns
and ochres
that darken to black

and mud
beneath the brambles.
Trees hide their trunks

behind glistening ivy.
A breeze blows
and it is as if winter spoke

through music
as leaves drip
rehearsing random notes

on gravel, grass and stone.
Suddenly I know
a name calls to me –

Charles John Mullins,
Eldest Son of C.V. Mullins of Buenos Ayres,
come to rest in Llandaf.

Behind me,
and the trail I've left,

the river gushes on
gathering names.

Language Questions

My old language is new
because its soil is stilll new and flat.

I have scanned its flat face
raked its skin for nuggets
but have risen empty-handed after each attempt.

Maybe it is my old blood:
I am one more traveller
come South to sail the waterway of silver

but all I find is empty land,
and land, and more land.

The Birth of a Mother

> "There is no other way:
> Myth is the wound we leave
> in the time we have."
>
> Eavan Boland

Let us not forget
that I gave birth to my mother
and my daughter.
For nine days and six months
I waited for birth in hell.
My mother walked up and down
the street where I was last
seen. Past the flower shop
with its dark roses, violets,
lilies, and that rare narcissus,
its cupped petals smooth as fresh skin.

She stood on street corners, asked questions.
It was summer and the sun
scorched the shoppers, hurrying
about the after-Christmas sales.
Nobody'd seen or heard a thing.
It was no surprise. When I was
carried off the sun blinded.
The pavement under my feet
opened and all was darkness.
The city traffic deadened.
It was only a scream I heard.

Summer ended early that year,
the lassitude of the warm siesta hours,
the jasmine-scented air, the juice of peaches.
Damp moved in from the East in the River's breeze.
Mother sorrowed under lead-grey clouds.

In my new room, more like a ship's berth,
light weakened from day to day,
leaving me to grope around,
a woman growing blind.
I learnt to measure my body's growth
with new fingertips.
        *

He would come in the evenings,
he who had dazed sun
and summer that afternoon.
He'd sit on the edge of my bed,
talk to me about his trade,
who'd been brought in, who'd be next –
nobody like me, 'beauty fresh
as a spring day,' he'd say.
He knew of the six months ahead.
Said he didn't mind,
with him I'd be safe.

I talked of things I'd heard,
of sloping fields down South
at the foot of the Andes,
dappled in yellow with amancay,*
of the musk scent of white roses,
how they grew wild, earth being so live.
I pleaded to be sent there,
with the rest of them, that I'd be good,
would do as they said. But he shook
his head, 'while I'm here
you won't be carried off again.'

For nine days my mother searched for me.
She asked in churches, hospitals, homes,
in police stations, schools.
She denied her body bath and food.

Her wrinkles greyed in the city's soot.
The traffic-cloud thickened her hair,
blocked her lungs. She'd cover her head
with a shawl – its light blue
faded soon, turned the grey-white
of sky and cloud. On the tenth day
she headed for the heart of town.

If I could see her there, I would fail
to recognise this woman, both mother
and grandmother, grown prematurely old,
pacing up and down the Plaza,
flanked by white colonial arches,
tower, church, government houses,
skyline drawn by flag and cross,
witnesses of this city's history,

now they hear a woman's cry –

And I know
what she's always known
and been, and I, too
cherish this bond –
the silent blood-flow,
the patient feeding and growth,
the hope for birth
in each slight stir.

*

This is the moment I like best,
when light fades, shows no mercy.
(Beyond these walls the sky
is red, the first stars glare).
The square of yellow light
on my wall is a screen.
I see myself as I have been,

in a hurry with life.
Now I can slow down my tale.
This new place becomes me,
my eyes see what is past,
anticipate,
marking out the roads –

Because I see you out there, mother,
your time draws near,
you will learn my language
and when you hear my voice,
but fail to see me,
you will know I am
where you tried to spare me –
do not worry, you have said enough
against this,
myself,
this hatred of men.

> *That violence is not ours.*
> *Because the skin will be grazed,*
> *flesh flushed, torn, sucked,*
> *to feed new flesh,*
> *and blood is our monthly food.*

*

Now I will become his sister,
hold his hand
as we enter the room together.
Their faces will turn to mine.
I am to keep silence.

He speaks in a new voice.
I listen, as everyone else
around the oval table;
in the dim light
the evening mass echoes.

From his silence my eyes
peer hard into these women's faces:
I know them well.
Each one could be hers.
Their eyes tell me she has been
Here. If only. When. But we leave
soon and outside all is darkness
once more. The cold engine
rasps and starts and we begin
to move. My hands fall on my womb.

*

With words and acts denied
all this dimmed –
these visits to the church
where my mother had been –

because I knew, as mothers know,
she was found and led to the Holy Cross
and at first must have sat like me,
among people who have lost

people – an effigy of loss,
starved, yet fed by solitude,
moved by women who mother ghosts,
photographs on walls.

He is finding out things, he said.
I did not ask, learnt my role
of woman who listens –
at least he is not like others.

For life there was as thin
and threadbare as old cloth.

At least, my body
was covered.

And when the time came
he was husband, fathered
my daughter under his name,
though false.

I did not know then
the price for such kindness
or its word –
pomegranate

I say now, remember
skin, gauze-thin,
bleeding when plucked,
torn and I lifted it

to my lips, to kiss,
What is truly lost
will go unmourned –

birth did not come alone.
Every night there were
voices silenced and I knew
those were my sisters gone.

*

There is a word somewhere
to say what he's done –
deceit, guile, betrayal
are obvious choices.

Instead, I think of flowers,
cut and vased,

or even beyond that,
an un-flowering of sorts –

more like deflowering,
although he never laid hands on me.
They say he was in love.
All I know is his eyes

as he stood below me
and the escalator moved,
raising me to the world.

Mirroring Narratives

She speaks in his idiom now,
after all, *life is a bitch* when you don't,
leaves you waiting as the uncommitted
ciao ciao of his letter endings.
Italian is neutral ground, offering
a safe easiness while he sojourns on,
sacrificing family life for foreign
tongues and tribes which reassure
his freedom of male –

How long she'll last is a mystery.
For now she strips in the memory
of his body, rubs her skin
with the ashes of lost words –
soon she'll become urn,
a vessel for what's lost
between mirrors, between these stories
she weaves for him alone
which are not hers, but his.

What You Don't Expect To Find Here

Is the nakedness of the sand
offered to you by the receding tide –
ropes like dead worms
caught unaware after rain,
and dry boats, uncertain to stand still
as new statues on their pedestal.

Or to discover, as the wind stops
suddenly, a hollowness –
the ropes it played like strings
have ceased to move, the boats' masts
ended their metal toll and all

is empty space, a smooth expanse
of silence, no wind and no sea.

Kate North

Bistro

Behind the vibrant ink spots
that bubble around her,
sat in the immediate distance
like a beetle over a plate,
at the smallest table
cramped on the bistro's smallest chair
the shy lunch eater picks at a meal
bigger than her face.

Jabbing her cutlery like chop-sticks
into a Mediterranean work of art,
the waiter coughs
a disguised glance as he passes.

Reaching for the tea-pot
inspecting its bowels before she proceeds
to draw her drink in a long and elegant hand;
the woman looks taller for her efforts.

She's twitching each muscle in her neck
alternately, showing signs
that she's experiencing the new, alone.

This visitor crept into her unfamiliar,
my familiar space.
Not without permission
but with worry and eager witness.

Now she picks and inspects
like she's feeling that she shouldn't,
and is careful to place the napkin
as she found it, at the end of the meal.

My Life as a Weather Girl

When she died it started to rain
nature taking the obvious cue,
but I saw it the other way around,
when it rained she started to die.

The rain and the death happened
back-to-back, it's possible to see them
as one event. Two separate issues
living in each other's pockets.

I've seen rain get this treatment before,
being put in its place by ill-educated eco-warriors.
They don't do it with snow,
unless it's Christmas when it's traditional.

I've extracted the memory of each drop
from my brain with tweezers. I've imagined them all
falling in dignified observation, they don't land well.
Some even bounce off the pavement,
back to the skies in protest.

I've lost the argument now,
too many people weren't looking properly
and my version has grown ridiculous in their eyes.

I would like to say that the truth is mine and I am happy
for me
and sad for the others
who see rain as misery's lackey.
But now I must keep a detailed weather chart,
allowing me to prove
that when the number 23 bus crashed last weekend
the wind did not change direction
and there were no tremors through the planet's outer crust –
even when the driver was decapitated at the wheel.

Lying with Croeso

I am taking you out
and you are wearing language
like a dress. This is how you will talk
to me tonight.

You look like you can sing
and do so, as we travel over a border
to a recommended chef near an estuary.

Our pallets chatter.

After coffee you talk me through your skirts,
folds of garnish over pale limbs, tucked away limbs.
I am a moth plucking at threads.

I place myself carefully and we share
no words, only their beginnings.

Lying with Croeso II

You took me out
in silence, with a bare back
and dipping neck-line, clicking your heels
to my face for conversation.

You stared through the windscreen
all way there, tunneling through
the night to a lake I'd never heard of.

We ate there, excitedly.

I spoke about breath and about
friction, and the shapes that lips make
pronouncing vowels. You nodded.

I placed myself carefully
and we shared words but no beginnings.

Shoe

All that was left when they took a boy
away from the lush pasture filled with choirs of children
catching the ears of the vigilant for blocks around.

Worn at the heel and curled at the toe,
not even whole. Gashes through blue-brown leather,
slaver and tooth-score on the tongue.

Next to the burst ball
in an area of ground down grass
blades still falling and collecting in clumps.

Buckled, an impossible shape
sunning its sole in front of a crowd
mumbling and cursing around the object.

The item that survived
to testify, a remark,
made by a mad dog, a statement
left on the green.

Twenty Minutes on the London Eye

This is a fantasy.

The city is about me
when you are on me with your lunar smile
and gossipy calves,
we revolve through our ordeal
a display.

We trip the commuter's gaze like always
on the morning skyline
and feign embarrassment only after we have finished.
This is a present.

A sentimental ride
blossoming angles of skin
into, through and out of ourselves.

White coin in the clouds
jaunty as a cartwheel unbound
from her carriage.

Advice on Heavy Petting in Coastal Areas

Have yourself a healthy serving
of pie and chips and gravy
then splash it over your face.
Smear it across your torso
in brown and lumpy smudges.

Get a close friend
to lick at you, like a platter
of delicate veal served cold
and fresh in the afternoon's air.

Make sure this is done in public
on a bandstand in a park,
on a pier or an esplanade.

But – don't stick your tongue down anybody's throat,
not even as an hors d'oeuvre.
Only rude people do that.

Postcard I didn't like to send

I am now in the valley for the summer
and await your arrival.
I write this from the boulder we pushed near the rockery
last year,
in order to catch the breeze for writing.

I am looking to the cottage,
the shutters in need of paint, the torn insect screen.
The door hangs lower than before, forced.

The dogs on the porch are like hardened-black beef
warped in the heat and infested
with yellow movement in their bullet holes.

Inside, the cocktail bar has been disgraced to shards
scattering through the lounge
and tracing about the house in glints.

There is no
light nor food nor sound,
only a stench that the lavender patch cannot compete with.

The bathroom is fouled
the linoleum is dangerous with mud and crap.
I have spent the morning
scrubbing lipstick graffiti from our walls.

The weather is still and the neighbours are away.

John Jones

stone stable midnight

outside this darkness
distant suns blink time
through missing slates

here I watch
my stallion's eyes
that from the dark
watch mine like suns

the space between us
ever more important
than the space apart

in the hedgerow, something . . .

there is a different sound
between the languid bee
held within a haze
of nectar
        and the quick probing
            of fat flies snared
                within the scent
                    of rotting meat

        seems that flowers
aren't as fast as flesh
even in decay

sedimentary

Mesolithic marks
  that once
were muddy traces
  now revealed
by the storm's tongue
how
three
crossed
these flats
their footfalls
felt like fingers
      floundering
          for fish
one man
his imprint
deeper on the left
carries something long
forgotten
  his son
my son's age
scampers through
the edge of a wetland
the same but unlike ours
      and sometime
in this distant passing
they stopped
to sound
to gather
in footprints
some words
that must have been
much greater than a grunt

John Jones

         we find
there's something here
of language
that's borne

by wind
by tide
by some chance to live
perhaps to die
a little
away
from town
tacked out
for the rock
or the hard place
I sometimes cross like souls
and talk
most
leave words
imprinted on my mind
  in town it's different
in town
we have
advanced
to the dark age
a composite tongue
distilled from celluloid
where any conversation
seems minute
too shallow to sip liquid
from a gathering of small rain

the sea lion circus

I love you
for asking
   me
      to bare my soul
                ata stomp
         and so close to the sea

         but my poems aren't fish
         nor likely to be

starting out

yearling
in a wheelbarrow
       and some book
             my wife has
reading the words
by torch-light

and me
a kneeling god
  forearm tight
in the slime of birth
  looking for life
 in the wet darkness

John Jones

seventh wave

there is no god
   but this
reflection
  we are
the smile backs
the tear keepers
surveyors of sorrow
diamonds on a viper's back
we are the light givers
the cracks between
dark clouds
heavy
in a stubborn sky
we are the changing winds
shakers of trees
makers
of a blown kiss
we are the seventh wave
shore bound bringers
of the silent dead
that leave their
voice in empty shells
while the devil breeds
in stagnant pools
we are restless
the keepers of all things
changing
but the will
to see ourselves
beyond corruption

between cats' eyes

bird
imitating
  leaf
half trapped
taps
at tarmac
a crow
down-road
pecks
at splattered
offerings
my tyre tread
obliterates one
while the other
blows free

Mike McNamara

Donald Brown's Grave, Christchurch

If there are tears that must be shed for you,
violent man in your peeling cloth,
I cannot be the one who cries.
In the back streets of your drunken world,
where oaken-cornered gypsies snag,
shirt-tail exposed and squeezed-on shoes,
you would have stayed the same.

On this hour, as I hear the chimes,
in some rundown basement hovel,
with your sense-struck street survival,
base techniques and bristled face,
there you would be, tumbling, fighting,
fornicating in an unknowing haze
of bitterness, and weariness belying years.
Or outside, in the windy street,
oblivious to cold and pain,
casting shadows on the walls with
your greasy hair and mad-eyed oaths.

And I am sure you would have stayed the same,
here, with the sunshine on broken weeds,
an epitaph to wasted years.
Light through trees, from sky to stone,
plays on my enquiring son; on my
impatient dog, and wooden sword.

Donald Brown's Grave Revisited

Tomorrow, I'll be as old as you,
the unsacred mysteries you praised
as the hard, back-street High Priest;
they too are mine.
I couldn't make your stone, still hanging;
darkest Pill, ten years and Christchurch Hill
have maimed me.

Yeah, the dog's still with me, though my son has gone –
no time for talking to
bones of men he never knew, besides,
one dead drunk called is clearly deaf enough.

Carl was killed last May,
full of apple, on the Alway Block.
Kenny Jay drowned, pimping in the Docks,
his chick, the tall Italian, split
for Neath, tattooed legs and all.

I've closed my eyes, coasting, as I've slipped on down.

Since you went, I've had a stint
in the City, University, but didn't stay.
They liked those lines about you; sharp
tutors talked of sympathy, underdogs, destiny.
They'd have felt the same, of course,
if they'd crossed you, drunk and bloodied
On some misspent Giro night.

A God's found Gail.
I hear her pray for you and me,
the living, dying, dead. The undead.
Though spring's come round again,
and ripe globes swell on young green trees,
our home still reeks of old neglect.

I'm aging in the flesh alone,
as old as when the Christ went up on
one fruitless, spring-time tree.

I'm sitting in the old men's bars,
and young boys play our past unruly roles
in streets and alleys, clubs and pubs;
I've seen us, through windows dark with years,
time and time again.
There's no retrieving mislaid hours
from sudden slipped-by days
we passed, but passing,
truly could have lived.

A Child's Brief Benediction

This world colours me in somebody. Something.
Nobody that I know.
Who decrees that I was meant to be
the chiaroscuro portrait, colourless to me.
Hush! There was a child once, silent
and blond; he raced on the Ballygally sands,
brown and raceless. No other land had risen yet
beyond the waves, past school-book views of Africa,
America, Australia. No self-division
in a child's One World.

Country walls, grey and dry, ran only from Antrim
to Glenarm. Christ died on the bad man's cross
for all the girls and boys, as my Granny whispered
prayers to the Sacred Heart, balanced
by Dan McCormick's scything gaze.

Saviour of Ulster, late of Judæa, crushed on Calvary Hill.
Dan McCormick, late of Carncastle, lost in Larne
raised fist and family, foundering

in the shadow of the grey Mill Brae.

A for Apple. M for Mother, days of wonder,
turning cheeks and tea-time-tears to joy.
If men, rising from Brouthshane understood
the value, would our towns be burning?

I have not laughed in years. Like Dan, like Christ.
Men can't erase their boyhood footprints in the sand.
The Sacred Heart of Jesus, straight-faced,
Fighting Dan McCormick, cold-eyed.

I lay embattled on the scullery floor:
comics, catechisms, pictures, preachings
read as one. Superman, Jesus, Santa.

Once I prayed to them all, a child's brief benediction.
To heroes seen and unseen, known, unknown, needed.
Beyond the walls of Antrim, that run through Glenarm
to Armagh, Belfast, Bogside and beyond,
no gods or heroes, known, unknown, still needed, now remain.

Adrift in the Asylum

Picture a sky in shades of faded denim blue,
forever 1972, a voice singing 'Vincent' on the radio
softly, and I, incarcerated in brought-from-home-pyjamas,
blow seventeen candles to darkness,
the heir to seventeen summers and Sun Valley roll-ups
in the asylum. Painting apocalyptic horizons and
destinations for the therapist's inaccurate chart,
washed up by the rhododendrons, fag-paper thin flotsam
in Levis with naked sunburnt feet and sandals,
a potential rumred Nelson, anaesthetized,
brutalized, a vacant lot, cast adrift for decades
from the calm and on-course, the neither hot nor cold.
Lost in acid flashbacks where The Star of the Sea sits,

her face obscured behind a veil of sleek black hair,

beside my bed, and whispers disconcertingly clear
above Jock the alcoholic's Greek alphabet recitals
her terrible lifetime indictment. . .
'This ship of fools sails to no harbour'.

And I, unread, untutored, a fermenting brew
of pop culture, wholly Roman lies, True Crime, Marvel comics,
detention, pitch and toss, one night stands, acne,
Parade, Cockade, amphetamines, barbiturates and
Spotlight bitter. The dichotomy of Good and Bad,
accepted or rejected, perceived in chosen haunts or length of
                                                              hair,
straight or stoned; no Fisher King but a sullen sprat
dredged from the nets that trawled the gutter,
police cells and O.D. wards,
too many, too much, too soon to take true bearings
on The Trout, Old Green, The Globe; universal
docking grounds for wrecked abusers, prison fodder,
scurvied bum boys with Borstal spots and tattooed swollen hands
or the bastards of idealism who see no ships, broken, bent
                                                    and crooked
in the long, shanghaiing, limp arms of the law.

The foul-breathed familiar of addiction laughs at myths
in mustard coloured corridors, spits on 'The Sunflowers',
curses 'The Empty Chair'. Manics, depressives,
alcoholics, neurotics, junkies, psychotics. . .
high flying, flying high schizophrenics, plotting their course
at the non compos mentis canteen.
Witless pressed gangs, sectioned walking shadows,
victims of the chemical cosh we sink like small fry
down towards the darkest weir where crazed drowning sailors
moan in hand-me-down sartorial sadness,
purged of mental mutineers and stripped of star or steerage,
sad captains, ancient and insane mariners

who eye the east for a slumbering sun,
toothless, dribbling husks with bulging, lunar, nightwatch eyes.
Laughing at silent asides, the keyless pursers of cryptic
                                                    monologues,
word-salad profundities and meaningless, mindless mirth
sail their sound and fury ships
to unmarked destinations through howling inner storms.

Redlilac Dream
After Paul Celan

Kiss me, arabesque,
I am the willow weeping
tears for your tenderness,
tears for your forgiveness. . .
we cannot say goodbye
you and I, you must not say
'I will let you go'.

In the redlilac field I carried him,
a heavy weight, my son of blood,
the players of games played on,
I saw you distant, young,
your graveyard smile on
milky black lips.
If the road leads only to
the place of death
how can I bear him long?

There are flowers growing in the prison.
Today the sun shines. You and I walk free.

Steve Prescott

Plastering

With your heart in it,
getting things done,
beyond simple questioning
it holds answers.
Days stretch out into cold,
flat expanses, develop
into a game of balance
and levels, before dissolving
in a soapy aftermath.

Steel against slurry-soft movement,
arm and back talking up a sweaty
logic, a blistered sense,
it's a bucket and stick philosophy.

Whistle while you work
the one good song you know,
taking your time over things
as fast as you can go
in a square dance,
a jig of life,
a magic show
turning pink milk
into hard silk,

and all this is the world's
open secret, it's all around you
in the manual intelligence
of each well considered
ceiling and wall.

Trouble

Always like that,
she could make people
go against the grain,
like when I got talked into
burning down Tuffnel's shed
or that time Danny stole
a car for her. She loved it,
though she cried later,
and I hadn't seen her for years
until I caught someone
smiling side-long at me
in the hotel bar.
She was with the manager
and he was drunk,
a hotel manager,
Tuesday drunk.

Gardening

Hiccuping bees blither along
the predestined routes
of their aimless ways, ignoring
Mrs Jones' murdering Tom
as he pours silently away
down the garden wall to smuggle
another bundle of feathers into the
cellar.

And as the grieving sparrows complain
and the garden hisses in collusion,
I lie beneath you and feel
the terrible strength of instinct.

The Bigger Picture

Unless one of my brothers
was involved the news
didn't really bother us much,
though I do remember
the Pope getting shot,
(us being Catholic and all),
and when Chernobyl went up
we were watching telly
while having our tea
and even the old man stopped
eating, scratched his belly
and said 'Sheesh' before asking
for the salt. World events
don't come much bigger than that.

Hand-me-downs

It is cool in here, a muffled creosote atmosphere.
They have asked me to take away your things;
nice they said, to think of someone using them.

I run my finger along boxes and jars,
pick over tools, handles worn by time in your hands.
There is not much of use. Seedlings near the window

vote against your going; they are clocks you set in motion.
A forgotten net of bulbs push green blades towards
the light. They make me think of fish, suffocating in air.

I settle on a pair of gloves, try them for size.
In one I find the dried husk of a wasp, a relic,
reminding me suddenly of heat.

Paint

Before easy chemical
colour was conversation
between man and material.
Hue derived from substance:
crushed beetle shell,
If needy ground stones and burnt earth.
When wealthy, ground Lapis
Lazuli and finest nut oil.
The steady poisons of
lead and cobalt complementing
oxidised gifts of
zinc and verdigris.
And one produced
from the urine of cows
fed only mango leaves.
The process and result
a yellow it's own
most singular word.

Recovery

There are visitations, faces appearing
on the blurred edges of sleep.
They bring new names to remember,
the stone of each word weighing
heavy in her mouth.

Each day emerges unassembled.
So many things to learn;
between balance of knife and fork
the long journey of a cup
from table to mouth,
daily rituals of refusing doors,
and the cruel conundrum of stairs.

Lost hours are punctuated
with endless moments
where her gaze mines
the unconditional knowledge
of a flower petal, rain, blue.

Fished like trinkets from a pocket,
she carefully measures the precious
nuances of each fractured memory.
Slowly, she will arrange them into use,
make something to put her name to,
or when she notices us,
offer as a gift to strangers.

Brothers

He has grazes on his face,
a split lip. I don't ask;
raw knuckles are narrative enough.
Warders and high ceilings
smother any chance of privacy.
Our whispers scatter out
across the room, counterpoint
to a low, familial drone.
'I've been working out' he says.
It shows. This broad, lean man,
clean shaven in blue,
threading out an hour
through yellowed fingers.
Then an abrupt scud of chairs,
the awkwardness of not touching,
of knowing we have never touched.
And his shape drifting away
through the room, children
spinning like tops across the floor.

Zoë Skoulding

Feathers

No-one ever knew. A wreck, we thought,
a long way out at sea. We never found

another body, or any other trace;
the sea was a blank.

A foreigner, we were sure of it:
his mouth didn't look the right shape

to have spoken our language.
When we turned him over we found

scorch marks on his back as if
he had escaped a burning ship;

what clothes he wore were soaked in wax,
congealed about him, cracked

where he'd been buffeted. Candles, we thought.
Maybe frantic signalling at night,

emergency or lost direction. The feathers
we never understood, except

if we imagined a host of angels
abandoning the ship,

hot loops of their wings
beating towards the sun

or a cargo of geese
all let loose at the moment

when hope was lost.

Parachutist

While Armstrong and Aldrin take those giant steps,
images crackle and blur through space to reach
you on your tenth birthday, kneeling there

in shreds of wrapping paper, your head fizzing
with plans and calculations. You observe them,
coiled by the television, feeling

every sinew fighting gravity.
Life is going to be like this: the future
will be weightless and belong to you.

In your hands you flex the plastic joints
of your new Action Man, with parachute.
You can hardly wait to cross the bridge,

climb that monument, the column raised
in memory of the man who lost his leg
at Waterloo. When you reach the base

you crick your neck to see it as a rocket,
the Marquess a lonely astronaut who gazes
far across the Menai Straits which he's

about to leave. You disappear inside,
bound up the spiral stairs so fast that you are
dizzied, whirl up through the darkness till you

burst into sunshine. You reach high
and let your parachutist fall, circle,
drift into the trees, land out of sight.

My Father's Binoculars

Those black-ringed worlds would never fit together
as landscapes juddered, heavy on my nose.

Catching glimpses of blurred bracken, rocks,
trees where I least expected them, I scanned

the layers of blue, looking for you. Space
reeled in and out of focus; sky wobbled

uncertainly, or it might have been water.
I steadied my hands, inhaling stale leather,

the scuffed strap round my neck in case
I dropped them. Your military binoculars,

made to arrow to the point of threat
or target distant silhouettes, left me

giddy on the beach. Then all at once
there you are, sailing far out at sea,

so close that I can see the gleam of mackerel
in your hands. I move and the sea is empty.

Trans-Siberian 1927

His letter from Shanghai, his seventh, reaches
Tientsin at dawn. *Dearest Madge...*Already
he's forgotten what he's written. He polishes
his shoes until he sees his face in them.

No coin here is genuine unless it's stamped.
There are three kinds of dollar which are often

counterfeit. Real Chinese money is the tael,
a silver, boat-shaped coin one never sees.

From Ulan-Ude to Irkutsk, the train
circles Baikal. Fishing trawlers plumb
transparency, cut through clouds which swim
the surface. The letter's curling in its sack.

There are chits for almost everything,
even laid out in the pews at church -
you fill in what you want to give -
end of the month they all come home to roost.

From Novosibirsk, empty trees
give way to empty trees. Her letter
(if only you could see the roses now)
number five, crosses his at Omsk.

Last night we went out to the Carlton. You buy
a book of tickets, give one for each dance
to the hostesses, mostly Russian girls.
I danced with one who wore her hair like yours.

A guard leafs through *Pravda*. The train pulls
slowly out of Moscow, on to Paris.
Young soldiers watch themselves dissolve
through glass into cyrillic blurs.

The Tailor of Ulm

Conversation was a low insect hum.
The mayor and his guests arrived in a flutter of robes,
gleams of sunlight on silk. Expectation
floated on the currents of our breath;
the winged man flew, alone against the sky.

We'd seen his careful little stitches,
the industrious construction of the frame
and wanted him to thread his way through blue,
rising till the Danube was a neat seam far below.

We saw him flying east forever, almost heard
the chimes of distant towers, the babble of foreign tongues.

His plummet broke the spell. The crowd unravelled,
disappointed at his tangles in the water.
Someone was muttering about the last time
our city reached into the heavens: that great cathedral spire
which they embroidered on the sky until
gravity tore gashes in it, ripped it down long ago.
As we took our tiny pathways home, something in us
rose like the dreams of ants, that dream of building it again.

By the Time He Gets to Nant y Benglog

By the time he gets to Nant y Benglog
I'll be shifting my head on the pillow,
feeling the weight of dreams unclog
as a stream of ants comes pouring through
the bleached rim of my left eye.

By the time he gets to Pentrefoelas
the blue light from the curtains will be
turning me green. As dawn uncoils
I'll look down from this body
sprawling here, soaring and steep.

By the time he gets to Cerrigydrudion
I'll sink further into sleep,
filling his space like a stone

dropped into water: soundless, deep,
leaving ring on ring on the surface.

By the time he gets to Froncysyllte
I'll be reaching the crossing-place
as the spool of night begins to stutter
and snap. He'll feel the threads between us
stretch as thin as B roads on his map.

Buchenwald
Gustav Klimt, 1905.

Beech Forest was an innocent name
when you chose it, light as slender trees
spattered with gold, patterning a clear horizon.

Loading your brush with crimson
to fleck dead leaves into the ground, there was
no reason why you should have seen
how that colour might look
as it seeped into earth.

Painting the luminous grey verticals
you were not thinking of fifty-six thousand ghosts,
or the roots of the trees and how they might
probe and shatter concrete chambers,
tangle with hidden bones;

the rhythm of lines is the sound of a waltz,
not the slow chug of trains to their termination.

This is an entirely different forest, where the beeches
dance blindly to the sun and only one dark trunk
leans forward, a stained word.

Adela's Elephant

Here comes that elephant again, swaying
across the lawn as if she owned the place.
Grasmere has never seen the like!

Her flank's a wall of stone which blocks the view
I used to to love. I can't get far enough
away to focus. The doctor's hands are kind;

they made me think of yours, of skin on skin
dissolving everything. He soothes
the elephant. Don't ask me how she got here:

too vast, too painted, she looks in on me
as if I'm hollow tracery, a figure
on a frieze, as if she's trying to see

the real me, who's hidden in a cave,
who has become a cave, where echo on echo's
calling someone else's name.

The Bridge
Berlin, 2000.

It's not so much what's there as what isn't:
the strip of forest where the trees have not yet grown,
the concrete bridge connecting roads which have
vanished under leaves.

The absence runs on, stopping at nothing,
cutting through roads and rivers, pavements and houses,
sometimes visible as a cobbled suture,
a seam between the world as it was
and the city as it is;

it's a faultline through Potsdamer Platz
where the buildings have pushed down roots
faster than trees, binding old rifts with
steel threads and sky-high glass.

At dusk, the bridge is an apparition in the woods.
A sound like the skitting of dry leaves becomes
a shaken spray can. The bridge
is the only thing that's left to paint,
but the lone boy has no slogans, nothing more to say,
except to make his sign for himself
over and over again.

The Aztecs of Cwm Llan

Light is obsidian knives, the sun in splinters
on a pyramid of slate; copper
stains the scree to sunset
from some forgotten
ripping out of hearts.

At the ruins of the temple of the cwm
Madoc's people chat in fluent Nahuatl.

Gladstone dodders on the rock, bringing
tears to the eyes of quarrymen
while everybody sings

and goes on singing, mouths
full of earth.

Rosie Dee

At it from the wrong end

If we could only walk through life backwards,
Squirm, slimy, from the muddy womb at ninety,
Your spouse ready caught and wandering by your side,
Rocky noses growing smaller
With each pace.

Then I would savour that toast, well buttered,
Knowing I'd paid for my sins. I'd do wine well
And bask in a body, uncrumpling.
Finding more voices, fuller music,
Distant horizons in every step.
Discarding the specs at forty.

Like summer my days would sprout minutes.
My thoughts, less tainted by the knowledge of yesterday,
Would sag, baggily, towards that glorious clay,
That childhood, before the inner pit is dug,
When the world outside is a collage
Of close ups: of smooth and rough.

The path, laid out before me, would have the logic,
The safety of a detective novel
Read from the last page to the first.
Maybe even puberty could be fun
If you were to go at it
From the wrong end.

Rosie Dee

Charlie Paints His Egg

Unfertilised and expelled
from an oval womb
into a black factory.
I am carried into corners
in your warm, sweaty palms.

I am baptised in treated water,
shockingly cold, and scrubbed.
My swaddling robe of excrement;
the cosy cloak of my mother's chicken shit
whirlpooled into a torrent of dark imaginings.

I am a face wiped clean, for the time being,
by your plump, your amateur hands.
As Father you lean, from your great height,
to place a kiss, to breathe a gentle death,
that blows the hole at the centre of me.

And master, clasping my voluptuous girth,
You slap wet lips and stroke hair.
You cast eyes with endless clones,
like my new and painted face,
caught in the slippery sheen of your cornea.

I am watching, mocked
by an indelible smile,
while glib fists whisk,
while hands stained by Smarties
the red of my mother's blood,
beat
and eat
my yolk.

And you let me loose
and I roll, down this rough slope,
erratically.

The Farmer and Her Cardigan

The Girls

Like the Tupperware skies it hung grey and itchy
upon your shoulders. Buttons, large and black as coal,
cold embers of a time before we were born.
The fuzz of woolly hooks like a kindling halo,
caught marvellous thoughts dangling in the air,
tempted our sticky fingers, our apple stickers.

We hummed to your wing, huddling
in a mass of limbs. You, in a sheep-cloaked fatness
letting us suckle, when we were small and round.
But now, skinny and redundant as the cardigan
on the Oxfam pile, we are torn from you
by the rough, glinting teeth of a carnivorous city.

The Ewes

You are bitter. I can see. You look into my eyes at dawn,
burst red vessels like the frail wisps of your cardigan

                                                        against
the yellow rising sky. We spend our days in green fields.
A flock of mothers in a slow, grazing mourning.
Working our jaws to the rhythm of the wind.

I am not bitter, though you came to us in the guise of a

                                                        mother
in your muddied boots, your pseudo-skin. We trusted you.
Until our babies, gutted and basted, were served up with
parsnips and rosemary at a table with too many chairs.

The Lover

I am round and firm before your hands
unravel me. Pull at a thread hanging.
And click clicking, your plastic fingers
twist me, from a safe distance, knit me
into some pattern in your head.
Your double glazed eyes shattered into four,
fragmented and focussed on my little stitches,
like pixels, superimposed on their screen.

I do not resist, and you pour me
like an undone ocean,
and I lap at your palms.

And now, at night, I dangle
in a dark closet, while you lie cold.
And every dawn, drawn tight
round your heavy shoulders,
smothering your lardy breasts,
I scratch like a cruel memory.

Following the electric pulses of your brain
Moving as you move, I am
an enveloping shadow.
While you fondle my button at the belly,
And my arms squeeze yours,
And you think of me, warm.

Waiting Tables

Waiting tables. Collecting crockery and spoons,
tea stained and clattering like empty mussel shells,
fine ceramics, in the corner of a beach.
Ruffled by waves, chatter, other people's
tidal lives, swelling and rolling by.

A couple by the window, as they are, every week.
His words trickle and drip like the tacky, stainless
steel teapots. And she holds her head, a tilted cup,
filling and over spilling with thoughts of her own.
I call them June and Bob and avert my eyes when they
                                              look up.

Their woolly arms brush, a static electricity of two
cardigans, haloed against the sun blinded window.
They are smudged silhouettes. And they drink their tea
with thermal gloves on, dropping scone crumbs from dry
                                              lips,
their pale faces against a gun metal sky scribbled

with black backed gulls. When they leave she puts on her
                                              kagoul
though it is not raining. And they're gone, like the birds,
to negotiate some untrodden space, where they might
or might not exist. And the table is left empty like
a glimmering coin in a dark purse. I pull at my skirt, and
                                              polish it.

When I take her mug it is left imprinted.
Maroon lipstick on the rim, skin cracked
and peeling, the pattern of her lower lip like
wood grain. A satellite photo of a weather system.
Milky rivers in a delta of blood red sand.

And I am glad that the cheap washing liquid will not rinse
the mark, which speaks of a different hand. Swathed in a
                                              silk glove
and clasping the fine handle of a cup. A memory which
                                              mists
at the elbow. A ghost, sitting on the rim of my baby-eyed
                                              focus,
and glazed, like the glass of the bathroom window.

When I take her order I call her Mother.
But she smiles and I laugh.

And bring them extra cream and hand-wash their cutlery.

In the beginning there were canals

And from the
Water sprung boats

And from the
Boats people

And from the
People pubs

And from the
Pubs drink

And from the
Drink music

And from the
Music sprung motion

And from the
Motion lovers

And from the
Lovers' waters

Sprung me.

Lisa Mansell

from St. Teilo

I: Requiem

By seven thirty
October night sucks up the heat on Woodville road.
I wait for you outside St. Teilo's
Leaning back against crumble cracked lime
That holds windows that once gripped glass
But now hang empty behind
The gilt dipped tips of iron railings.
The hydrangea sheds her cornflake petals
While I look for you amid a carnival of revellers
Wearing illuminated devil horns
That dance on the dark in the distance
From which you emerge half enveloped
Encumbered with cold.
St Teilo stands above us,
A face scraped from old stone
Sinews stretching as he speaks:
"Come into this place of pillars
That paint the organs pipes,
Poised
Placid
In their marble pearl skins"
His speech ebbs away
Silenced under concert 'A'
That ushers us in from hypodermic rain.

You and I walk down the aisle
And you steady me as my spiked heels stick
In the grates on the floor,
And I click-clack against tiles.

I am dressed in a cream canvas coat
And you hide vampiric teeth in your pocket
In preparation for the party.
We pray that God turns his cheek
And not watch as intently as Teilo.
Solo soprano ascends the stairs up to the pulpit
Accompanied by a homophonic hum of orchestra.
The conductors beat deals her cue
Cutting the condensing cold.
Bassoon and basset horn unfold
And creep in to catch the basses bellow
Below contralto cantabile:
Requiem aeternam dona eis domine.
The tenors take their tune
Before the solo bass inflates his chest,
A robins breast,
His larynx spilling sostenuto:
Tuba mirum spargens sorum.

Moments after the music ends,
Just before the applause,
Old notes resound around the rafters—-
An ecclesiastical acoustic
To wake spirit's song from sleep.
I bring out my horns from hiding,
Throw off my cream coloured coat.
You pop in your plastic fangs
Freckled with flecks of fluff from your pocket.
We open the door
Let in the October night
That sucks the song onto the street.
This vacuumed sound flirts around the feet of old St.
Teilo.
I strike his stare as we disappear into the nine-thirty night,
And I ask him:
Why do I feel guilty for not loving God?

I Won't Send Roses

You must have pushed so hard
To crack the crust of leaves
That roofed your wrestling roots.
Stem and stamen stick through earth
To stand up in the sun
Where sundials tick long shadows on the soil.
You strip off the dark
That hangs like skirts around your stalk
That clings to leaves that breathe the light,
Drizzling drops of dust on dirt
From which you have fought free.

He must have been so proud
To find you sitting fresh
Against the curdled cawl
Of twigs and tarnished bits of tin.
He brought his secateurs
And shaved them sharp against your skin,
Splicing strips of green.
The scalpel blade that nicked your neck
Swept swift:
The flower's picked.

I should have been so pleased
To take you as a gift,
To stand you in the sun
That glares through double glass,
Staring scorches on your flesh,
Branding burns on bowing boughs.
He cups me close
And I cliché:
"You really shouldn't have...".
The sap on his hands stings my skin
As you wither in water and wilt.

Digging

My spade split something softer than the soil
Something rotting
Putrid in the ground.
Looks like you're dead
Stagnant
Fetid,
So I shift you aside with my shovel,
Your epidermises undress.
A palimpsest of vests
That fall off and peel away
Slipping off in swelter.
And becomes exposed your seed
Fighting from folds that form your flesh:
Another onion
For a cliché around a Frenchman's neck.
The seed I'll sow amid
The arid leaves of shed skin,
To rot again
Like you,
To leave again
Another onion
Another onion
Another onion.

Jellyfish

In July,
Jellyfish cobble the bay,
Sand grouts channels in between
Surfboard standing stones
That circle ceremonial fires,
And the razor rocks
Slice the sea, rip the tide
In half at the headland.
They slash the jellyfish too.

C-Shanty

My favourite letter is 'C'
It is curly-cut
Like a crook of a contra-bassoon
Deep sea diving in Britten's Sea Symphony,
And the seagulls seesaw on its surface.
Their feet are sore and
I see their chilblains raw.
For Britain's sea is cold cast salt
Hung in chilly water.
Standing on the stave I saw also middle 'C'
It precedes the letter 'D'.
Diddley diddley dee.

Deborah Chivers

Test

I had to go for a cytology test.
I'd put it off for months, as you do.
The nurse said OK, here's the drill;
slip off your panties,
pop on the couch,
and assume the position.
Oh, and try to relax.
She was quite a comedienne.
Bending down between my legs,
she was about to ask
if I'd booked my summer hols yet,
when instead she stood back quickly.
Hello, she breathed,
I thought I'd seen most things in my time,
but this takes the biscuit.
I sat up.
Is anything wrong, I asked.
Well, don't freak, she said,
but I see two old people up there.
What do they look like? I said.
She bent to have another look,
and extricate her instrument.
The woman's wearing white sandals,
and those icky sockette things;
the old guy's waving a newspaper.
Did you notice which one? I asked.
She sighed and had another shifty.
The Telegraph, she said turning away.
That's my mum and dad I said.
Any messages?

The nurse was trying to keep her voice casual.
Your mum's saying something
about a strong cup of tea
and a sandwich.
I can't say I blame her.
What does my dad say? I asked.
She was at the sink by now, washing her hands.
All your dad wants
she said, is his mac.

Weird Hole

I was in town with Wendy.
As we came out of Marks and Spencer's
she was updating me
on the progress
of her embarrassing rash,
when I heard this screeching sound
and the pavement opened
right in front of my feet.
Naturally, I stopped and peered in.
There was a rush of damp air.
I could hear water plinking.
Some bloke warbled up from far below,
come and join me, it's party-time down here.
I thought it sounded like a pretty silent party.
As if, I called back,
and edged around the wobbling stones.
I could use some fags, he cried,
sounding crest-fallen.
I don't smoke, I yelled over my shoulder,
and hurried to catch up with Wendy.
Wow Wendy, I said,
how unexpected, you know,
the way that hole just appeared
in front of M and S.
She turned and frowned at me.
What hole? she said.

What Happens

This is the one
where she runs
down a corridor
holding her children's
soft, waxy hands,
and Elvis is crooning
are you lonesome tonight,
and her long skirts
are bulky and noisy,
like that cheap sleeping-bag
she bought from a discount store.

In her ears, the sound
of rushing water.
Underfoot,
plush red carpet shrinks
from the skirting boards,
revealing two strips
of a glittering,
murderous, full-pelt river.
She peers down, down
to where long, grinny sharks flick.
They are upholstered
in the very same material
as her new lounge curtains,
but their teeth are
Richard-Attenborough sharky ones.
They snap their jaws peckishly,
rolling over and over.

Both children
slip from her grip
and shoot away
beneath the water's green surface.

Their huge eyes blink slowly,
their blond hair waves goodbye.
As they disappear
they wag baby index fingers.
This is what happens, they yell,
this is what happens
to mothers who

Her Week

Eat quarter of a bowl
of seafood pasta;
the mussels look like
tiny excised cunts.
Note to self:
no interest now felt
about eating that type of thing.
Also all three tomato-hued prawns
could have been
severed human ears.

Buy pair of fishnet tights,
colour: aubergine, apparently.
They rupture as yanked on.
Instep still painful from prongs of plug.
For future ref:
false nails, though feminine,
are detrimental
to delicate fabrics.
Uncomfortably bleak truth:
medium hosiery
now proving inadequate;
sizing's a minefield.

Deborah Chivers

Break down and weep
sitting in strobey, twilit cinema
listening to the soundtrack
on a Jaguar advert:
Roy-Orbison-meets-Edith-Piaf-type voice.
Interesting sum –
fast cars plus certain music
plus cinema snacks
invariably equal brief despair.
Question: could it have been
the popcorn that smelt farty?

Perform daily power-walk.
In bedraggled park,
hide behind bald tree
and greedily watch poodle
run in circles like black athletic lamb,
a good long way
from unappreciative owner.
Pat on self's back;
super-human restraint employed
in struggle not to scoop up dog,
conceal under
voluminous wooly,
and leg it home.

Awaken at three-thirty AM.
Bedroom curtains
blocks of orange neon.
Slide out of bed,
pick up large pebble,
invaluable as door-stop.
Drop it on his exposed foot
to rouse.
Then hold said pebble
in two hands above head,

firmly announcing,
I know this sounds harsh,
but fuck off
until that thing gets better.
Repeat to oneself
each night on retiring:
decide it,
sort it,
feel like a new woman.

Wings

I followed her upstairs
and saw piles of rubbish
spread across the floorboards.
It's been hard
to find the time she said.
Now I'm fixing these together
with strands of my dear children's hair.
I've been collecting it from their pillows
over the years.
See, his springy, blond locks
for weightlessness,
hers, straight and black,
for strength.
I've used many things
in this construction.
Two types of chain,
fine and heavy,
perfect for the harness;
old irons, shelves from the oven;
thinnest shavings of skin
from the back of the one I loved.
I did it in the night,
he never woke.

Gold rings; perfume bottles;
pieces of the mirror
I smashed seven years ago;
the arms of my father's glasses;
the tip of the tongue
my mother lied with;
the head of the doll
my sister stole, perfect for a prow-head;
silk slips, dried roses, baby teeth.
This crocheted shawl; love letters,
all used for ornament.
I've utilised certain extracts from my diaries;
grey, white, black days, a few crimson,
to provide much needed lift.
Be my witness, she said:
whatever the wind's direction,
I fly out tonight.

Heron

I received one
smelling of frog-spawn.
It was full of feathers
that brushed my bare shoulders
like warm ferns,
and thin, funnily-hinged legs;
I had a feeling of being trampled.
There was a snaky shape
always weaving about.
I kept seeing shining, flat eyes.

Eventually, I made it to morning,
stretched my arms, yawned,
and saw a heron
sitting in the wide-open bedroom window.

Its compact head
pushed the curtain to one side,
its neck described a question mark.
Webbed feet, the colour of old egg-yolks,
hung down in rubbery folds
against the radiator.
Giving me one serious look,
then pivoting its head outwards,
she launched off inelegantly.
Breast feathers like flakes of new sky
floated on to the carpet.
A breeze blew in from the river
and lifted my fringe.

Then I noticed:
next to me on the bed,
in a nest of ripped pillows,
sat a huge pale-blue egg.
I put my ear to the still-warm smoothness
and heard a knocking sound,
someone calling my name.
A piece of shell fell on the duvet.
I put my eye to the chink.
Is that you? I said.

The Knowledge

She whispered:
our mother's cunt
is like the eye of a lizard,
bleared and slow,
sunk in a goose-flesh socket.
At times it drips amber tears
that burn small holes
in the edges of our mummy's skirts.

You've observed
those lacy patterns in the hems?
Well, now you know.

She told me:
Our father's prick
is as long as a dingo's
and easily as whippy;
When his hind legs fold,
it drags on the floor.
You've seen how daddy winces
when he hunkers down
to play with us?
Well, now you know.

She said:
Your seed and mine,
black as two olive stones,
dropped from our father's ear
into our mother's silver throat
while she sang to him
one cat-calling night.
You've heard those
raspy sounds she makes?
We ripped her cords
when we were born.
So now you know.

Insect

She's lying in an old, oak bed,
but really this is about centipedes.
The room's festooned with them.
They smell like licorice,
only more rooty.

Some have beards,
some are sterner than others.
One has the face of Dean Martin,
but they all make her shudder,
even the one thin as a French bean
who abseils from the lampshade,
a beetle gripped between his jaws
like a rose.

As centipedes drop out of the curtains
they sound like falling All-Bran.
Soon they writhe in shiny
mounds on the floor-boards.
She thinks she'll scoop them up
but nothing is to hand.

The mounds gradually quieten down.
It seems they are snoozing.
For this, at least, she's grateful.
As the room dims,
(a nest of young centipedes
has covered the only light-bulb like a hat),
she discovers a twelve-inch granddaddy
on her pillow.
She's paralysed of course,
but mentally she shrinks away.
He rears up and weaves
like a creaky vermilion cobra
in front of her narrowed eyes,
works his way around
between the pillow and her bare neck.
His touch is like Velcro.
As he snags her hair,
and deposits something gunky
underneath her jaw,

she whispers: I will not accept
I wear you like a scarf.
And anyway, this is just a dream.

He tightens his grip
when he arrives in front of her nose again,
then tunnels through her flesh,
just above the Adam's-apple.
He's inching up her windpipe.
Her mouth flies open.
Where her tongue was, there he is.
Come on boys,
he says in a voice like wet toadstools
to the glinting crowds of centipedes
watching breathlessly around her prone body,
help yourselves.

Hello?

Once, I choked in the street
on a slender grey bone.
Retching,
I ran to a phone-box
and called you.

Hello? you said,
from your office
in another city
forty miles away.

At the time,
as I clutched the handset
and knelt coughing bubbles of blood,
I felt you could help.

Instep

She was fifteen,
climbing rocks with friends.
Squirming as barnacles
pierced the balls of her feet,
she slipped down the slime
of bottle-green pools,
grazed her shin
on a stretch of molluscs,
lay on her front
and watched purple sea-things
open and close,
open and close.

Then she fell,
cut her instep deeply.
It didn't hurt or bleed,
she was so cold.
They carried her back,
settled her with cushions,
and went swimming.

Feeling light-headed,
the beach-sounds fading,
she cradled her foot
in both chilled hands
and gingerly pulled apart
the whitening wound to look,
then held her breath,
shocked at how like
a sea-creature
she was inside.

Deborah Chivers

The Otamak Eat Earth

And tell about the usefulness of doubting.
They call me 'traveller without a shadow'.
Take heed, they say,
all animals celebrate the full moon.
The jaguar is our shaman.
Flowers take flight:
crimson, flame and dark-wine.
The Otamak show me harmless,
black-skinned vipers
who feed on venomous snakes.
Above us the forest exhales oxygen.
The Otamak hold spears, bend low,
request forgiveness
from fish with fins like human hands.

We take only to fill our bellies, they sing.
We are all one: hungry, naked, grieving.
They hold up brother stone,
smash brittle fish skulls,
at sunset roast dense flesh
on wet cinnamon twigs.
They bring spiky palm leaves,
poisoned with Curare,
show how to bind them round
elbows and wrists.
We mortally wound our enemies
in hand-to-hand combat.
We give the captured man
his sister's daughter, they say.
Then he is slaughtered and eaten.

In the rainy season
I listen to the wild boar herds
grind their teeth and snore.

The Otamak explain
how to make a shelter
of palm hearts and aspidistra.
They tell me it is lucky to host many bats in them,
laughing behind their hands.
Surrounded by frogs big as boxer puppies
I tell the Otamak stories about snow.
The Otamak speak words,
mouths flickering in the fire-light.
They say my way back is barred.

Richard Gwyn

Memory of Drowning

He had a pirate's knack
of laughing loudly
in the wrong place,
a tendency to gluttony,
hostility to random strangers.
He pandered to the lesser gods,
rejoiced in the misfortunes
of his many enemies.
How he swaggered,
swigging rum in low tavernas,
concealed blade itching
like a barnacle against his thigh,
in thrall to the violence
of the sea. And if you racked
his brains, you'd find
shrimps and sea-slugs,
anemones, restless hippocampi
lodging in his memory,
contented squatters
in the caverns of
what passed for thought.
His lips contrived an opiate
of shipwreck stories,
each one beginning well,
but ending incoherently.
He carried his failures
like a sack of looted gold,
as much a part of him
as kelp on his sea-boots
or the memory of drowning.

Arrival at Vilarig in a Storm

Purple clouds amassing
over fields of wheat:
a swollen pomegranate
split with fullness. Watch!
From her pulsing womb
the waters break.
Tubers, wild and questing,
disturbed antennae,
spring from her damp
vegetable mound.
Thunder cracks the walls
of tolerable sound.
My daughters, undiminished,
stamp a bull dance
in the rain. Gods
alerted to our coming
turn the quaking night:
lightning, wind and waterfall.
We enter, set a fire.
Shadows leap and
hover at our backs,
penetrate the wall.
We sit by hearthside,
smoke, and tell our tales.
It is this way
that myths begin:
a storm, the thirsty ground,
gifts of fruit and grain.
Our talk elicits
boundaries of night.
Outside the wind and
scorching rain: inside
the alchemy of firelight.

Richard Gwyn

New Year's Journey

My wish that New Years' Day - to ride wild horses
over sunlit hillsides. What I got was misery, abandonment,
and chaos. I loved it, all the suffering and heartbleed,

Humbling moments in the shadow of the god: and pain,
the haloed pain of tragedy - there was not enough that was
enough;
it was never quite enough. And then you wanted more.

Trips through winter islands, marooned on Amorgos,
the ferry anchored to the island for a fortnight's storm,
And when we leave, young Nelson told us,

So long waiting, we will drag the island with us.
Islands, islands, each one with its secrets; each one viewed
through rain-swept glass in sea-lashed ports.

Kasia, Nelson, Declan and myself, with Kasia's babies
made a crew of six; the travelling winter circus.
Set a precedent, I told the others as we started out from Athens:

You see, a lot had happened in a little time, our heads were
full of Kasia's kidnap, articles of occult interest,
Artaud's madness, a girl who danced when she was sad,

And other ceremonials observed in a sprawling cemetery
at the city's edge, where the crimson paint shrieked
on the marble of her family vault: *Antigone, Antigone.*

On the boat to Paros, Kasia called for brandy "to feed my
Slavic soul". I sniggered at such self-parody, as the ship
pitched like a drunkard through the January swell.

On Amorgos we slept rough, the Wicklow boy and me:
he had to cut his sleeping bag to make a spread for two.

I was wakened by a crone who screamed "You'll die you'll die"-

And realised that we were buried in a snowfall. Frozen, we
huddled by that widow's woodstove, numb to any world
                                                    beyond
our island, yet we had a mission raging in our blood.

In Paros on a toilet wall I found more evidence, this time
attributed to Lorca: "I come from the countryside and refuse
to believe that man is the most important thing alive".

And there it ended. Or ought to have. The final boat trip,
ticketless, we spent below decks, boozing with the crew,
and then returned to freezing Athens. Night that followed

Sleepless night. What passed for mind so brandy-stained
there were submerged cathedrals in my eyes, songs
of drowning women in my throat. And then, one afternoon

I crossed Syntagma, and stopping at a signal felt a tug
upon the sleeve; an instant of impossible reflection.
I shuddered, knowing that my call had come before

My time, and then moved on. The rounds of energy
that reckless travel requires were seizing up, and I retired
to a gloomy hostel, stayed in bed, read cold war thrillers,

Evenings talking with a schizophrenic Samiot named George
who worked in a biscuit factory with forty Cretan women.
"Barbarians!" he sneered, "they all the time make play with
                                                    me".

Kasia and Nelson married, live in Warsaw, have six kids.
I passed the Wicklow boy years later, playing whistle in the
                                                    metro.
His eyes were gone; what lay behind them also.

Modes of Travel

Serge travelled the pilgrim's way to
Compostela with his crippled dog

the dog had two broken legs
from two separate motor accidents

Serge loved the dog and travelled
with a push-cart on wheels

into the cart went blankets
food and clothing

into the cart went the dog when his
two good legs would not take him further

On Ithaka I met a man who travelled with a coffin
he'd fixed the coffin onto bicycle wheels
and carried his possessions inside

at night he slept in his coffin
if it rained he pulled down the lid

he was prepared for any eventuality

September 20, 1989

On the steps facing
the cathedral of Lugo
sat a crowd of beggars.

Among them a
reincarnation of Pope
Pius IV, blind drunk,

Was attempting to
recount, through the
fog of centuries

The exact purpose
of reconvening
The Council of Trent.

Camels Trotting

The soul travels at the speed of a trotting camel.
Nowadays, when humans venture any distance, they
choose a mode of transport significantly faster. The result?
Lost souls, everywhere. Once when I flew from Athens to
London, stayed ten days, and then returned, I reckoned
that I passed my camel over Serbia, going in the opposite
direction. From the parched membranes of a feigned
amnesia I conjured cowled faces against a starlit sky, folds
of black silk, tufts of animal fur, dried blood, stale sweat,
the cold night air of the desert crossing. The rhythm of
this memory is that of a human heartbeat. The images
retained by the eye are formed at exactly the right speed,
and fade in time for the next one. Food is chewed and
swallowed in accordance with precise instructions. Water
only is drunk, and preciously conserved.
The pernicious attributes of a godless world are simply
unimagined. Names are kept secret. Animal images
predominate. The deeper you dig, more beasties come at
you. Everything has its animal corollary.

Lifting the Virgin

Her job is to keep the church clean, arrange the flowers, change the candles. At midday she cooks a meal for the priest. But her main concern is the well-being of the alabaster statues, especially the virgin.

Last week, she tells me, they had to lift the statue of the virgin, move her awhile. "You can't imagine how much she weighed", she smiles, as though discussing a defiant but beloved child. The wind has stopped. Everything is quiet. I walk with the priest to the village bar, and drink a *fino*. Afterwards, in the square, the children gather round, playing and chatting, as though they have known me all their lives. I am a stranger, who has walked into this tiny place and soon will wander on. The woman in the church, the priest, the sky, the children, the little square with its tree and two swings. A conspiracy of nouns. But the effect is of a flow between one thing and the next, on a journey that has lost all points of reference and offers only the salvation of continuity. Lifting this lifesize model of the virgin provides a challenge to all that is unchanging in a village on a plain. She was so heavy. You can't imagine.

In the Palace

I wanted to tell you my secret water story
but the truth is, it is all waste
and watery talk, like this wading
through disgusting slop water,
corridors and alleyways waterlogged,
caves and passages carrying
their desultory flotsam from room to room.
It's as though we inhabited a palace
where the currency of courtliness
was sodden, washed-up remains,
old garments, rotted food, corpses,
and the king's throne spinning
slowly through the flood
like a wooden-limbed crustacean,
rats jumping from an arm-rest
to the bobbing chandelier,
snakes shimmering across the surface
like troublesome movements
in the mind at dawn.
All our energies are taken up
with wading waist-deep, simply wading
through this disastrous hall,
while the king himself lies drunk
by the window in the highest tower,
singing shanties to the propped-up
carcass of his queen.

Richard Gwyn

Hunger for Salt

Will I remember you in the dull yellow light,
as a fish that enters my mouth, as a virus
that enters my blood, as a fear that enters my belly?
Will I remember you as a catastrophe
tearing between my legs, fine teeth slitting my lip,
tongue touched with salt my tongue was crazy for?
You never confessed to those little thefts:
my mother's ring, the statue from Knossos,
the locket I kept for the hair of children
we never had. I see you, come to steal my bones,
small teeth so white, a necklace of coloured stones,
clams and mussel shells around your waist,
an ankle chain of emeralds. But now you have gone
back to the sea, I can forgive your cruelty,
your violent moods, your plots of revenge,
remembering instead the brush of your skin
on mine, the way you looked at me that afternoon
in the sea cave, gulls clamouring outside,
a crowd of angry creditors in a world otherwise
gone terribly quiet. And you, nestling in
the white sand, caught in the nets I wove
with a devout sobriety, turned utterly to salt.

John Short

Antonio Agujetas

Into that fetid cavern
filled with *fino*
and perfume
comes the gangster comic,
Oblique-faced
phantom of tangibility
he straddles a chair backwards,
points a diamond finger
at the crowd.
Cracked voice slants
out in wry comment,
eagle eye
and finger dancing
over the tourist Japanese,
over young lads
and old women.
His guitarist warms
becomes better
and fluent,
hypnotic
in deep *Soleá*.
Antonio stands up
sidles to the wine,
his angular shoulders
a vision of honesty
and dishonesty
in precarious
inscrutable
balance.

John Short

Disappointment

On May the 3rd 1976
Brother O'Leary has bad news
for the boys.

The school trip to Barcelona
set for the 18th
has been cancelled.

Up half the night inventing
excuses, because he found out
just in time

that the Plaza Real
and lower Ramblas
is a teeming cattle market
of whores and queens

and that on this account
the hotel there
is not suitable
for a Catholic holiday.

A narrow escape, he thinks,
though his palms are sweating,
his collar chafes and the peroration
of his speech rings false.

But the boys, momentarily
stunned by this meteor
of disappointment, soon forget
and turn their attentions

to other things, not pondering
or thinking to question
the vague explanations.

Mr Percy Gedling

Mr Percy Gedling was a taxi driver
and a practical joker.
Drove the kids home from school
and smeared their front doors
with butter.

Had a cocktail bar in his bedroom
and a penchant for walking
on barrels
under the horse chestnut tree.
Raced his Cortina at 88 mph
down the dual carriageway
then one day fell
sideways off the stairs
(they had no banister).

After his first heart attack
at age sixty something
the laughing man smiled no more
and when he died
there was no one to fleece the kids
by flogging them conkers.

However, he visited me in a dream.
Covered in tattoos and wearing
a woman's wig, he said:
"Don't tell anyone I'm here.
Just having a quick look
around."

Big Ted in Barcelona

Don't blabber on the balcony,
he counseled, or be euphemistic
at the escritoire.

He had an apartment on the Calle Princesa,
rented with the proceeds from
the Dalí sketches that he'd found
in a hotel trash-can in New York.

Owned an enormous dog, had
hung around with Leary and Ginsberg
and told nasty stories of the gay 50's.

Did water-lilies wet on wet
and butterflies, which paid his bar bills.
Said he knew an aristocrat in Sitges,
who painted pictures with his prick.

Was writing an epic novel of a thousand pages
to denigrate his enemies, while going up Montjuíc
for nocturnal liaisons.

Would leave his typewriter in the oven
for safekeeping, until one night it melted.

Bohemio trasnochador, where are you now?
Some say in Venezuela, or back in jail
for forgery, or blackmailing
a bishop in Baltimore.

The last time I saw you, sixty years of age
and nearly two metres tall,
you were loping down to the soup kitchen

to muscle in among the bums
and pretend to say your prayers
over the steaming *caldo*

while privately despising geraniums
and contending that the Jews of
Europe gassed themselves.

The Abandoned Treasure of Esterrai D'Aneu

Empty room
in an empty house.
I'm lying on my back
in the debris.
Above me the crumbling ceiling
supports solid silver stems
and three engraved white globes.

In the street below
a herd of cows is passing.
Iron bells
make dull, artless music
in the freezing morning air.

By my head
a bottle of plundered milk
and a can of water.
I have only an ill-defined
sense of loss
and a desire
to leave this place.

But one day
I shall return
with a step-ladder.

John Short

Narbonne (La Zone)

I met a man from Armenia
sitting on a bench.
He offered me beer
and played his radio too loud.
Then came a crying woman
With a purple eye
and Vladimir wrapped
his blanket around her
saying:
with Vladimir no problem.
I'm *Católico, auténtico*,
like Jesus.
Next came the crying woman's
gypsy boyfriend with a knife
and mean intentions.
A balding maniac
spitting through the gaps
between his teeth,
but he stayed for beer
and talked to me in Spanish
folding away his knife
and looking at the Armenian
said:
that's not a human being.

Dracula meets The Devil

I got tired of
popping up
like a frozen carp
and not cutting my nails. . .
decided to try
a drop of Old Nick
(they say variety
is the spice
of Life: what then
constitutes
the spice of Death?)
I could have
staked my existence
I'd hate the taste
but one gets used
to anything.
I went out
and punctured a few snakes,
then, despairing,
considered myself
equally at variance
with the realm of Evil
as with that of Good.
I questioned how,
through the demon bottle,
men seek in vain
their better selves:
whatever they are not.
I saw that the path
to Hell begins with
a colourful and attractive
forest
and went back
         to the earth.

John Short

Pudding Island

The sky a sempiternal
blanket of grey.
Sleet lashed the window.

There was hypochondria
and deprivation
in the air.

We gazed at tabloid
images of idiot footballers
and politicians who looked
like cartoon characters.

He bought a pint of mild
in a barrel glass
and a pizza
topped with baked beans.

I observed this with alarm.
"Surely nothing so perverted
and barbaric", I said,
"could exist in Europe?"

"This isn't Europe", he retorted,
with a sly inflection
and a glint of the eye.
"It's ENGLAND".

Waiting for the Albanians

What are we waiting for, assembled
outside the Hotel *Tsímova*?

Why isn't anything happening
in the olive groves or on the building sites?
Why are the Greeks ignoring us,
drinking ouzo in the morning and pretending
that there's no work?

Because the Albanians aren't coming today,
so what's the point of bothering
to do anything at the moment?
Once the Albanians are back
they'll put everything in order.

Why has Barba Yiorgos, veteran of a dozen
Maniot feuds, whose house is a tangle
of war relics, locked the door to the tower
and disappeared down the stony path
carrying a shepherd's crook?

Why is he not out walking with his elegant cane,
beautifully worked in silver and gold?
Things like that dazzle the Albanians.

Because now that they are gone
there's no need to impress. They liked finery:
sheep crooks, songs and rhetoric never
cut much ice with them.

They were only concerned with toil. They
got up too early and worked harder
for less money. They crept to the bosses
and smoked all our cigarettes.
They'd jabber on without respite
in their insufferable pidgin Greek.

When I came in from the fields one night
with my *axina*, Barba Petros moaned
that an Albanian could have cleared
twice as many trees.

And then one day, without warning,
The cops descended – some edict
from Athens must have filtered through.
I don't know exactly how it happened
but they rounded up the *Alvanes*
and took them all away.

The Greeks know that now they'll have to pay
a decent wage, something they cannot bear to do.
So they just sit in the kafeneion
and don't come to the hotel any more.

Night has fallen and the Albanians haven't come.
And some of the travellers just in from the border say
There are no Albanians any longer.

Now what's going to happen to us
without Albanians? They were, those people,
a kind of solution.

Rhian Saadat

The Passion of Abbot Bienaimé

In his dreams, Abbot Bienaimé floats on clouds of honey.
He presents his ideas to the brothers – talks of God
and a calling to explore the habits of bees.
'Love', he waxes, thinking in shades of nectar.

He denies them prayer, insists that matins
be devoted to the study of scent, and the hours
remaining spent in the gardens, with evensong
replaced by a silent Apericulture Hour.

Wood, willow, rush and clay, marble and glass
and even the humble canvas – all serve the abbot
in his unravelling. The bees will have none of his transparency,
and he is impatient for a vision of their sweet, interior life.

The brothers grow themselves a perfumed Eden, rosaries
of pollen. Bienaimé dissects the Cloche hive, the Scottish hive,
the Debeauvoy, the Nutt, and his nights begin to heave
with strange mantra, a worldy sweat.

He thinks of Judgement, the golden skin of native girls
coming to him at night. They have wings and smell of acorns,
and they bind him in moss and trembling flowers. He lures them
with his ambitions, dandles them in his woven bowers.

In their dreams, the brothers pass through the gates of heaven.
They pray that the abbot might find the inner strength he seeks,
to fight his recurring madness, return them all to their gentle cloisters,
return the crazed bees to their vacant oaks.

Passing Through

In this country, wood is scarce. People are poor,
but welcoming. A great thick door like this
is an emblem of wealth, the opening of which
might take forever since the transverse beams
must first be carefully dismantled. All this time

your host speaks no word,
and the only sounds are from the slow, careful
drawing of the bolts, and his inhaling, exhaling
you consider like some mnemonic greeting.

The frame around the door is an heirloom; see
the carvings – the growth of a world clinging
to its own roots. You can do that sort of thing
here. It is decorative, explaining the traditions
of those you meet, and it's the only reasoning
you encounter. And the small window? Yes,
they like to look out, take a peep at those
who come knocking. Nowadays, it doesn't
happen very often. Listen to that creak
of an opening. A thin stream of daylight

on daylight, and his beckoning hand. You step
in, and out again – straight through into
open country. You note his balanced sense
of out and in, without the necessary trappings.

He is smiling now, inviting you to sit with him,
take tea from a samovar steaming away
in the grass. But first, he locks the door again,
peers through the opening, smooths the wood.
Adds another leaf to the carving.

Sequoia

Double-trunk sequoia are the best
for building tree-shacks. You enter
head-first through the driftwood floor,
pulling yourself up by the elbows.

Some, coming here to visit, compare it
to being born again. Standing upright,
they say they can't wait for the wind
to starting blowing us, side to side. Usually,

they take their leave before it happens.
I've decided it's the noises they like –
the silence of a world made from nothing
that wasn't here already, the sigh of a wing,

the tree growing steadily around, higher now
than the hut itself, and singing its ancient lullaby.
they never mention the feathers though –
owl feathers spread evenly over the floor.

Just as well. Imagine explaining the crowd
that gathers here every stormy night – me
and my ancestors; we go back as far as the day
this tree took root, thrust its head skyward.

Table of Orientation

I have designed it as a temple, in three parts;
all that happened before birth, now, and eternity.
You are here, like me, just about in the middle.
I deliberately placed it under the old lime tree
so that travellers would know where to find it,
eat their sandwiches in peaceful surroundings

unaware that the remains of a murdered hermit
lie in clingfilm on a shelf in the local Mairie;
that the kink in the trunk, half-way up, is not
some quirkiness of nature.

We can see for miles, standing here, identify
every mountain range, locate the orchid fields,
dwell on the beauty of existence. Wanderers
have passed this way for hundreds of years,
stopping at the tree, locating where they were,
and where it was they wanted to be.

Weavers

I remember you as a weaver in Forqualquier,
the sign of a hand on the gate, at the end
of a long winding summer lane, and the small house

you had come to, years back, with a husband.
I remember him as a dervish, and thinking
what a sensible union yours must be – he

the weaver of movement, and you, the blender
of wools and silks, your creations – lucky charms
for the wearers. I bought a sunflower coat.

It's a little threadbare here and there, after all this years,
but I was anxious to wear it to visit you, to tell you
about the birds in my garden in Africa – describe

how the male weaves a nest of extraordinary skill,
and how the female inspects his handicraft before
confirming that she will mate with him.

Voyage of Discovery

'It is so easy, this road, that it may be travelled sleeping'
    (Mir Yahya Kashi)

There it was, our holiday craft, propped up on stilts
in the shadow of a lagoon, lilting into the afternoon sun,
its mainsail beckoning us to hurry,

as if its departure was imminent.

The soft creak and murmur of timber was soporific
and, stowing supplies, we slept, slept off the side-effects
of living, slept a steady drumming of cloth against the
spar.
When we stirred, we could see in all directions,
and our vessel was surrounded by water; it was a whale
of poon wood and coconut rope, sealed with oil and sugar.

The days and nights lost track of us. We took our bearings
with orange peel eased from the flesh in perfect spirals,
held in the palm, thrown to the foam. Our readings
revealed we were approaching the curled edges
of some magnificent adventure – we would dream it,

an ocean littered with horizons; waxed coracles
closing into perfect spheres, opening and riding the crest,

wave after wave after wave.

Chez Saltalamacchia

Will you take your elephant with the baldachin,
or without? Stirred from its long sleep
The creature will carry you far, night and day
when you order the optional accessories.

Perhaps you wish to travel further, in which case
could you not be tempted with a school of fish,
assorted sizes fired for a crackled glaze, flicked
tails, and dinner plate eyes, even for the gaze
of the minnows?

Where is it exactly you wish to go, and when?
We have a wonderful design for a cockerel, here,
crowing on and on, so that you never sleep.
If you're kind to him, he'll keep you awake
long enough to circle the world, and back again.

All your disused dreams may be stored here,
for no extra cost, in a very simple, lidded bowl.

Silk Route

There is sometimes, a deeper layer, hidden.

We came this far to find the savants, with stars
in our eyes. Now, they tell us they have gone,
long buried by the conquerors – tourists
in another time. We leave without paying

still looking for a crossroads, or a silkroute
leading to transparent hills where the locals,
they say, are made from a clay so fine
they remain invisible, unless held, turning

into the sun. We appreciate this feeling.
It is for this we came. We find, in its place,
a modern city, grinning through the night.
But, where are all the minarets?

Distant voices are urging us to worship –
these are Western tunes with an oriental beat.
We kneel, dig holes in the sand for dead phrases.
At first light, we shall head for the land of porcelain.

Letter to a Lover in a Gallery
(After Calder)

I'm not looking for a permanent romance, more a marriage
of bright and dark – or shapes of us – swaying out of shadows
to chime, lightly, against ourselves before gliding away again
and hanging, mid-breeze, taking the weight of lightness.

No frames to hold the visions in, no pieces calling *Look at me*!
I was seeking breathing holes in seeing, apertures in eyes –
small fissures to let essentials through – or optic pearls of being.

And then, imagine: suddenly there's this landslide of words,
spinning us in tangles across a polished floor, cartoon legs
rotating towards inevitable contact of finger tips, eyes casting
helplessly around for worlds we thought contained only
temple bells.

But of course, worse, you say, would be the standing still. we
might become fixed kisses, authorized positions for loving,
ambushed by a thousand eyes and waiting under cover of night
for a moment to come – in the form of a draft of air, perhaps –
when we might make for the vents,
take flight in silence.

Being Lost – Stage Five

*'Panic usually implies tearing around
or thrashing through the bush, but in
its earlier stages it is less frantic…'*
(W.G. Syrotuck, 1976)

I have never really missed that feeling of the ground
beneath my feet; halfway, and this scree provides
as good a place as any for sleep. And from here
I can just make out the land far below, one blue vein
of river and the quarry, a small red stain spilling over,
sliding out of focus. Volcanic now, I always imagined

it an indentation, on the borders of knowing home,
and flight. My porta-ledge sways through ninety degrees
and I fold my new clothes into neatly settled piles,
smooth the rolled tunnel of chrysalis silk.

Five thousand feet and swinging, base camp
is a shanty town of pulleys and rope, a vertical slant
against which the wind cracks and bounces its confusion.

Edgeless existence, and it isn't even cold. Tomorrow,
should the weather hold, I think I could reach the summit.

Hall of Mirrors

We would all prefer our lions to lie on fine large rugs.
this is the anteroom, and as far as any visitor may enter.
Please, be at ease – enjoy the elephants, the royal gazelles –
and the rhinoceros is yours for the evening. We dine

later, when there is so much more to uncover. Your business
is mapped in the heavens; we can smell it too, in your vodka.
Nothing is ever as it seems, and your ambassador's kind gift
of a chandelier doesn't fool us for one minute. Take a peek,

if you will, although our women are still in their quarters,
oiling their hair and brown bodies. Those secret rooms
have powers to multiply caresses – we can watch ourselves –
visit infinity. You, of course, will not participate. Our home

is yours, but only as far as this doorstop. Solid gold,
and welcoming.

Camel Deal

Tails, we lost, they kept the jeep, the maps;
we took the camels anyway,
rode into the sunset keeping, best we could
for first-timers, the galloping in time
to the women's drums. It would never do
to appear as amateurs, lost in sand and
strange rhythms.

Our ululations were as good as any
ever heard this side of East; a ten second blast
could ripple a sand dune at ten paces,
and the beasts could be trained, we imagined,
to speak our languages, or at least to answer
simple proddings.

But the sun sank, and we, still riding on, passing
caravanserai, oases, dunes unsung and laughing
at the sight of us, nodding to sleep in the low arc
of our camel skins, their humps vacated, freed
to juggle again to that self-made beat, our feet
at odds with the balance, soles braced against
the freezing drone of night.

Rhian Saadat

Larger than Life

One degree of latitude for each dream of the Tropics.
The arrival of light, and we alter course – chuck dates
at the Weddell seals. These are our Julian days –
and through them we can peek at pleats of buzzing frazil-
ice shot with chaotic pattern. Sundogs howl their crystal
                                                    rainbows
and seawater spouts, sky high.

Larger than life, they warned us; try to slip past the jellyfish.
But there she looms – in a space shaped from imagining –
metabolism spun across snowmelted time – the sea her air,
the ceiling of ice her planet, and us, orbiting in the wake
of her waltzing drift. She is every colour yet to be created

flounced organza membranes, ripple-silk lips, and a
filigree trail of substance more akin to memories, before birth,
of a journey that began in being here and seeing this,
understanding only that we are the shadows, bead-black,
and she, the myth.

World's End

Yabrai Yanchang, last village before the desert
and the lake is the garnet of halophyte. The land is quartz,
its reach so high, you'd be right to mistake it for mountains,
each dune piling itself over the next, creating tombs
from their ancestors' hills – their ripples buried echoes
of their own haunted past. The old woman, Diudiu,
sees the ghost each evening – they rise from the fire
as she sits with the goats.

The new year is designated Year of the Mountain.
Diudiu knows nothing of this. In her recurring dreams
there are visions of a distant city. It is flat and shiny
and she would be forced to leave her flock behind.
Wind blows sand to settle in her shelter; in the Spring
she will sweep it back, remind the spirits of strange birds
she has seen, flying fast, beyond the edge of the lake.

Sarah Corbett

The Witch Bag

Remember me. I am the woman
who shook her fisted nipples
at the moon,
bearing down the dark streets
that could not take her.

My face broke in two
as I ate its bright cheek,
my hands sudden as marshlight
held before me
into the dark nights that followed.

I am the woman who flew
not only in her dreams,
but remembered the spell as she woke
and hunted sighs like ticks,
dipping and turning as she went.

That woman, weightless thing,
thin as pond moss,
blacker than the pond's black belly.
She hooks its clammy limbs around her own
and sucks the water into herself.

That woman, without a world,
who goes hopping with one boot
between twilights,
a bagful of grave treasures
lost and lost again -

mask of hair, milk tooth,
heel-bone, blood-purse, name.

Black Crow Woman

Hear me singing.
My songs are crueller than mountain songs
trapped in their cold snows.

I have a shadow so deep
it would eat you, or worry your sleep
to madness so that you would eat

your own children to be free of me.

The hour never turns that I do not know
how it lays its weight on babies
until they cannot breathe

and must bleed out their hearts from little holes,

how it calls the birds to fall from the air
to feed the starving pavements

and chokes every skyline with its black hands.

Draw my deaths from me, one by one.
My bones are a graveyard of bones
where the dead pile their grievances.

They circle as the crows circle the tired day,
calling and calling for the night to relieve them.

I will show you what a dark word love is,

how generous it is to suffer,
laying your body as a bridge
for others to pass into morning.

Sarah Corbett

Feast

Five blue swans you brought me,
patterned finely as porcelain,
carved, you said, from regret,
sorrow, grief, despair; except the last
being a thing lost, a shadow.

They stood on your wrists,
your shoulders, the fifth paddled
your back, flourished lapis wings,
curled the ess of their necks -
your aura, your sex, your language.

Your heart was a plume, oiled
and resistant. Showing me this,
sadness silvered your cheeks,
a river of pearls in your hands
where the birds fed delicately.

You cut off their heads,
hung them to dry where they danced
in the wind - five abandoned dresses -
served their breasts with jewels
dug from their throats.

You fattened with pride as I feasted,
my fingers claggy with juice,
my mouth huge with desire.
When I had finished I spat out pearls,
wove the bones in my hair.

Green Rose

First, I was tenderly young.
Second, I believed myself empty of sex.
So when I sickened, ballooned,
I thought it was fear breaking
out of its egg at last.

Your father kicked down the door,
dragged me by the hair
and raped me in the cold backyard.
How was I to know of your heat
in that bitter pod inside?

When, at twelve weeks, I heard
of your presence, your Thumbelina
arms, legs, spine perfecting
in the walnut shell of my womb,
the black earth bloomed.

OK, I engineered your death,
but woke after wanting you back,
searched all the rubbish bins
in all the backyards from here to Liverpool,
broke my teeth at the clinic walls.

You are my daughter of the green rose,
you demand water daily. You root,
put out leaves to catch my rain.
Your closed buds never flower
but hold tight the colour of my crime.

Sarah Corbett

Ocyrrhoe Becomes A Horse

She had not been content merely to learn her father's arts
But could reveal in prophecy the secrets of the fates.
         Ovid: Metamorphoses, Book 2

The words spoke themselves.
I heard my father's death
ring from his lips, forsaw my own fate
as if a great iron bell had uttered.

In the burn of the far hills
my maiden self is departing.
By the river where my mother
washed her hair and bore me, I am changing –

my flush skin becomes my bright hide,
my neck stretches towards the sun,
my hands push and harden.
The beast stirs, it paces in my blood,

my tongue thickens on consonants;
the wind, sharp in my throat,
carries the imprint of water,
the plain's constant notation.

I am lost, unhappy daughter,
who could see what she could not change,
to the fever that rankles in my bones,
the earth's thunder.

The Night Before Your Funeral

I made love to my husband
in a stranger's bed, felt the sorrow balloon
in my mouth, which I refused to open.
My unborn was wakeful; he turned and kicked,
weighed heavily upon me.

I took the dream as a sign. *Release me*,
you said. Your face was a mask
of worry and sadness.
You were at the chapel window
restless for the wings you had been promised.

I had not seen you for a year.
I could imagine you beachcombing
or sketching the roots of a tree,
sunlight shattering through leaves,
your hands a mosaic

and I wanted most to touch your hands,
your muscular hands edgy
with life, your father's hands trembling
as you reached in the dark
for my sleeping face.

But a glacier was moving
through me, settling its stones.
I had become earth. My eyes
darkened with silt and I heard only
the tapping of water far away,

the fact of your emaciated
body, your bird's chest cracked
open on the marble, the bruise
that must mean you now wear your heart
black, on the outside.

Starfish

Asleep you are a starfish,
your skin is submarine, your charged element.
You are skating, each finger
a water pearl balanced beneath the surface.

This is how I leave you,
suspended in the blue aria of your dream.
Like this my love floods in
and I could drown here, the sea filling my mouth.

Only unwatched can I release
this close harboured pain. I see light descend
through the water's cavern,
rain gently on your stippled belly.

Waiting as you dive for ocean bed,
your dark abyss, I keep the boat steady.
You are too deep to call back,
your eyes shells, your soul a luminous tail.

Bitter Fruit

My mother is an impostor.
She is at her looking glass,
every day I hear her speak to it,
she says, "mirror, mirror ..."

In the middle of the night
she is at my doorway,
a rain-cloud, a storm gathering.
her fingers spark in the darkness.

I know she wants my heart,
she is jealous as a fish.
she would eat it,
a fat berry darkening her lips.

I will run away.
I will live in the forest
learning to run on my hands,
love the smell of foxes and their ways,

hole up, like the beginning
of something – a pupa in a lace egg,
looking out at the world
from under a leaf.

If she finds me, I will change
into a pumpkin and poison her soup.
I will change into a mouse
and stampede all over her toes.

I will be a magnificent horse,
win prizes and be admired.
I will be a fairy princess,
wow everyone on the high wire with my loop the loop.

And she will dance on coals
to show her appreciation.
She will cut off her toes
to fit in my shoes.

lloyd robson

speed diary (extracts from)

1.

speedin & off 2tha 'dam tomorra. soon.

no great hit as yet jus a lotta snot & sizzle
bitta burn down throat backa mouth
bitta yaba wi sal
can't sit still
the search for stimulus.

a find for short time:
i wanna play at the minack or least read me stuff ona
stage edged by rock sea spray winkles stones whelks
& rescue helicopters from raf subzero station
landplot on some place cornwall.

need more.
fancy usin a passport page ta base a snort of icing nicely
whizzin now.

2.

am aware of writin at this paper
but feel not really thinkin hard no need ta search ta write.
jus waftin as ya may have noticed.

really v v excited *yes-i serious-i*
watching jimmy cliff swim his many rivers
"ana harda they come/as sure as the sun will shine"
ana bitta speed rubbed in me gum to add a little to me run
"i'm gonna get my share/what's mine".

3.

back 2tha minack: stone steps 2tha sea
                    blocksa verve & sinew slopin silent 2tha
                    coastal stage
                    white sat crumbled on mustard yellow
                    brown patterned square of paper wrap.
                    essence.
                    whizz waits without patience.

put down me pen 4tha rolled fiva & sniff thena spliff then
back 2tha film but back 2tha fiva first:
                    blue face sat white
                    edged shielded
                    royal duke face
                    nose poised 4 powda
                    purse lips
                    finga point ta powda powda
                    powdaplot of sensa
                    tional delight.
                    westbreezed bounty waves
rippling 2a sunglass hidden nostrilcavern wrapped yellow
brown pure coconut inside.

5.

foto'd me address so me cameras won't get lost
i want i need i deserve a lotta great harmonious happy
lovin fun
& memories of such
from this holiday of ours.

6.

writin's gettin harda & me cock weaka: i have small base
imaginins at 4.20 ina mornin.

spliffin constantly.

not bollocked at all except except standin jus then by tha chair
waitin ta climb me own personality ski lift ride
hangin swayin pylonwire
line over white dusty mountains.

sure
cock & stomach muscles tuggin but least jaws & teeth
underlyin un ungrindin der unground
keep that stale gum chewin.

7.

popped out 4a mo
opened door & stood in me yard.

light blue airforce grey but quiet

listenin to me flesh refillin & chillin 2tha bone
afta me piss
still shakin.

coupla birds

one i heard earlia/one i saw soarin wingsa monday mornin
blue awful airforce grey
fly from me bird not welcome here
fuckoff. this is not your day
4 noise.

today, today is monday
first ofa holiday
up allnight take tha bite outta sight kinda mornin

enterprise & adventure dawnin
so respect 2tha holiday maka
gogetta/jetsetta/firelighta/teethwhita/pleasurefighta/warria
of the goodtime ride
but bootless feet cold
i come inside from me yard.

8.

food?
nah, still billy whizzin
ridin me mornin of bizzarity
& this rolled 5pound note keeps on rollin back 2me
& me numba's nearly dead so jus a rizlablue roach of
matchsticklength & rolled & turned
& shaped by hand
tubular cardboard creation
yes-i!
grand.

little bitta spliff lefta carry me thro 2tha big blue line
whilin away tobacco ash & acme of caps
til i pullup/cruise/skank/kick downstream
lastdraw til tha burn & blue by flame & cardboardlungs
i should stub & be done but
exhale...

lloyd robson

sandinista tequila tabasco
the mayor go 3-course with aristo & amigo
from el real

chillipep *ah!* hot defrost *ah!* yellowbox meals
cashcrop equat *ah!*, sowta merik tequile
salt & citric gunship
splash tabasc
o!
combat gear.

back throat gone to overthrow
nost- guer- ril
coup d'état red as *the clash* go sandinist
blue as the argen
steer.

the voice of revolt

    all our mothers' tears

aztec volcay *no!* erupto toot sweet

       aristo! my arse bleeds!

aristo one unfunny gringo

       we owes you compadre

black shades-green beret-defoliate fields

    he wants heat i'll give him heeaa-sheeit!
    get the vatican mucho quick!

(saints bless this
unholy ring)

aristo & amigo turn the flame on el fugitive; the mayor
outside in...

letter from sissi (an extract)

we didn't wanna leave. both cryin (lips swollen, hair sungolden, lov glowin like a radialtyre takina coastal corna/orange stone/molten lava). if happiness was measurable by tears i wouldav cried til i ceased to exist but for tha sadness a leavin. the bus arrivin at twenty past, twenty five minutes to the airport fast, flyin *nothin* to be afraid of (planes take off a thousand times aday, but don't necessarily *land* when they get there).

we collected aar bags, loaded them onta the underbus shelf and pretended ta climb aboard (neitha of us wantin to be first, both expectin the otha ta kick outa burst an run for it, hide out at costa's an sell on aar passports) but we was the only pickup at this resort when irony of fuckin ironies, just as we're gettin there/just as we're convincin aarselves ta climb aboard/juss as tha driver an courier aar gettin bored waitin for us ta get it on aar alarm clock goes off (waves breakin from unda tha bus/sounds from within our suitcase/the tides flowin *out* towards us): hadta drag it out ta switch it off or else it wouldav mourned tha whole journey out (as if the two of us wasn't enuf). attention's upon us (we're still tryna notta cry/still cryin, written off as drunken taffs on holiday) when wallace really balls/i means *really* balls and i had ta/chose ta/ta carry her onta tha coach/chose ta/ta cuddle up an ta give some lov (i climbed the backseat all ta meself once we got outa town/befor me guts started throwin it all back upat me). waved to our haunts from tha backseat, cried in tha nite, tried ta sleep but the booze wouldn't hide tha fact we was goin ome. busride like a dream/nitemare/poison induced pseudo/halluco sound, me stomach like a sacka knees all jerkin round, i tried a fag ta bring me downta normal gravity, stub out not likin the clarity/stub out wi me barefooted toes on tha carpet, unaware of what i was doin (culture shock presumption too much ta handle).

and now i can see the airport an i don't wanta go. and i can see the airport, and i don't wanna go. and i can *seethe* becos i do not wanta go home.

i wanna stay here wi wallace in aar seafront apartment, eat melon, drink amstel an rosé an sun the resta aar lives away in perfect lov an unity away from stress an insecurities an if

ANY ONE

tries ta stop me/
and if *anyone* tries ta stop me

i'm liable ta cry again (i doan wanna go!), we really do not want ta go.

i'll send this from the airport (send it with your earlia postcard, i doan wanna go) and me an wallace may see you when we gess ome (she sends her lov) or not (we don't wanna go).

perfect company ina too-much world (we don't wanna go). perfect company inan ideal resort (ora heavyduty stressridden home? we doan wanna go/don't wanna be burdened by tha fuckers at all when all we wanna do is get on wi aar lives without havin ta *justify* ta every cunt that comes along/don't wanna wear *clothes* for tha statements sewn on/doan wanna live a life*style*/doan wanna put up wi judgement time every time we step outa our comfort zones/don't wanna hafta put up with the allknowin selfrighteous cunts at all, an that includes tha dole).

don't know what we're goin ta do but we do not wanna go home to what we left behind.

listen mate: *later.*

(not enuf lov intha normal world.
we do not wanta go home.)

our flight is *waitin.*

get over it get down to it jus doan let ya
mama catchya doin it doin it i told you that
boy doan know what his tongue's for he puts
it in places i ain't sure it should go what's he
doin with it now that's what i'd like to know...
(stammer rage, for short)

in bed
the two of us
the sheet *just* covering my cock
which rises in direct correlation to my eyes widening
as you promise the lot
offers i would be stupid to not accept...

    "if i Kould have *-eh -eh -anything?*

      "ifay *-*Kould have —*æny*thing...?

        "if -I -K -K -Kouldav -ENNY*thinggg*!?

"I'D *RRRIP*OUT MY *SSTU*-PID FFUCKIN TONGUE!!!
                                                 &
                                  *bbb*ury it
                                    in *you*"

                ....

      'people who stammer
     can keep it going for hours'
    (*bbb*umper sticker somewhere, surely)

compulse to repetition
(compose to repeat)
com cum pulse to repetish

my little carton of lush concentrate
my little tin of supe*(rrrrr)*
label me
ladle me
fold down
while i *bbb*ite gently
your *bbb*elly
(your eyes)
*bbb*urn my tongue on your
hot love lines
from your SPORRAN OF JOY
to my SPASM OF DESIRE
chords *grind...*

my *ddd*ysfluent tongue mutes
you:
                    "ooooh, don't speak now"

                                all our sticky nuances
                                        COLLIDE
                                make fluid sound
                                            &
                    our *ppp*uddle of love....

tongue tide lapse laps
all nite
all nite

...

Kerry-Lee Powell

Inhuman

They called from the hospital to say this time
You were really dying. I was fifteen, drunk,
Late home from the horror movie, my tongue
Swollen with kissing. I only ever visited you twice.

I'd seen so many deaths on the screen.
With knives, hockey masks, with cape and fangs.
Death didn't drain off into its lazy boy armchair,
As monotonous as your only lung's rasp.

Twice I stood by you, shifting from one
Leg to the other, my kindness stolen
From afternoon films: the woman with skin
Like milk, her breasts over the flattened soldier.

At the hospital I couldn't even pretend
I wanted to lean into you as I saw the others lean
And heave their grief out into kisses. I backed off,
But tried to look like a loved one, a human.

And then the glamour of describing a real
Dead body. It's no wonder your face
Visits my face in the mirror the least often.
My neglected grandfather, I would like you to have seen
That string of teenage suck-marks around my neck.
Your blood, my first romance.

Kerry-Lee Powell

Nothing

You were told the old reservoir was only
For drowning. As a dare you went in to the waist
Then had to dive for your lost change,
Or any other kind of twinkle that you never
Recovered. You plopped your stones in it.

You knew the afternoon train
Might come from a sudden silent nowhere
To take your head off but you offered it
Your last penny, your ears to the ground
Your mouth in the gravel until the sun
Was almost over.

You were warned the fires around the vacant lots
Would turn you into ashes but you heaped
A plastic chair you stole from the church hall
Breathed the smoke as it twisted into hooks
And wondered: who will be king?- not finally
The shape you made from dry leaves.

You were told the air past bed-time
Was full of unknowables. But you had faith
In the runaway emptiness, the skyline
A necklace of worried flashlights.
When they catch you, you say you saw
Heard, touched, have known nothing.
For the first time you believe it.

Night Vision

Where do you go with your night vision?
The moon is manned, off-limits.
The sky is all shooting stars.

New, Improved

Anubis strains on his lead outside the chemist's shop.
A dog-headed god set among
All the fossils of chewing gum.

His name, like a soothing cream for nether regions,
His yellow eyes - older than Jesus -

Measure the statistics of the passing throng.
He waits for Osiris, who flogs his goods in there:
Snake oil and death jars for liver and lung.

A special unguent for fear.

St Sebastian Ooh-La-La

Your first comeback was truly heroic
Sieved with wounds that never heal
You mouthed off again for God's sake to Diocletian
- and he was impressed -
And then had you cudgeled to death.

Renaissance hands re-arranged your drapings
Until, like a nudie magazine passed around at school
We could all see every hole.

We honour you by sequels
You were the Christ without the hype
Han Solo to Luke's Skywalker.
A heart-throb with mouths glued upon you;
Singing, like arrows, little pop-stars.

Patron saint of hits
And misses like me who have a thing about scars.
I blow you this, my kisses.

Kerry-Lee Powell

Nancy Drew

The attractive titian-haired teenage sleuth

You wanted them all in hell or behind bars.
Or at the least taken away by the police, the bad,
Who were forever haunted by what they never had
And always reaching for it with their many hands.

But the bad were also always kind to you:
Guiding you with echoes down crooked steps.
Planting their footprints in flowerbeds
Leaving you maps to places in the mouths of statues

Where ghosts would unwind their bedsheets,
And then detach their false moustaches,
Floorboards groan their secret clues
And a message in the hollow oak confirms:
All is as it seems in the land of no-metaphor.

What they really wanted all along was you.
Closets full of your warm breath,
Your mysterious presence everywhere.
Trunks full of your glorious hair.

Fandango

The hen-nighters set him off but didn't notice it,
The epileptic in the red suit.
It wasn't the strobe or the mirror-ball,
But the camera flash blue
Lighting up the dance-floor like an August storm.
And the bride-to-be, the bride-to-be
Dragging her tin-cans, her veil
Of condoms and iuds, her heavy head reeling
Between snaps. Then later, the developed set:
The thirty-six flailing red
Flashes of his arms, his many tongues, his legs.

The Ladies' Room is Always Haunted

The door blows in a background chorus.
Toilets flush, one after the other.
Heels on tiles make tap dances.
A virtuoso plays the hand-drier
Against the disembodied voices
'So anyway he just rolls me right over...'
And *'You should have seen her face when I told her'*
And *'What is wrong with men these days*
Do I need a Tshirt saying don't take me the wrong way...'
And *'I always shave my legs to keep my options open...'*
And *'I just, you know, need to have more fun...'*
– Sometimes it sounds like a musical.
Chopping up lines in your cubicle.

Stray Bullets

when is like where
might, once, have, with
all its other elses but
more sadly often ended
face down in never
and because of of and of
and all that gang of likelihoods
is still around is why I always
look over who and who's
shoulder as to what might
come, like if and only
sometimes wildly do together,
but much faster,
much harder than ever.

Hansel and Gretel II (the revenge of Hansel)

Who cannot help but admire the tactics of Hansel
That pint-sized strategician, who, in a time of famine
Marched with his head, not his belly
Laying his trail of crumbs
– Any ordinary starving child would have eaten them–
Then re-assessing the situation, re-traced his act in stones.
He wasted that witch – or perhaps she was just
An ordinary starving woman –
– and the gingerbread house just wishful thinking –
Avenged his birthright, eliminated the stepmother and her
ovaries.
Formed a truce with his weak-willed wood-cutter father,.
Before adopting his previous position. Son of. Sole Heir.

The Girls Who Work at the Make-up Counter

The girls who work at the make-up counter
Live holy lives and drink each hour
Seven glasses of rainwater.

The girls who work at the make-up counter
Live holy lives, and sleep in herbal blankets
Each night for seven hours.

The girls who work at the make-up counter
Live holy lives and wake up to paint
One sunrise on each eye.

André Stitt

Innocence

She phones him at work and
tells him the news, he can't
speak.
She sends him an email and
tells him about her belly, he undresses
and falls down the stairs.
She tells him she's evil, that
there is sun dried dust
turning
inside her body, that
parasites are burrowing
into her knees.

For days not so long ago
he recalled, something
golden, now morning
nausea, unable to eat.

For a time they thought
they could do anything, meet
any challenge, now
things hang tensile.

Let's pretend, she says,
let's pretend the future. . . he
holds his ear to the door, trying
hard to listen, trying
to feel this sacred
living thing growing, thinking
about someone else
who deserved better, and
the nature of turning, incapable
of life, incapable of
sacrifice.

Robinson & Cleaver 1944

Out the door
you run naked
to buy
my mother
a wire-haired
fox terrier

You build
a brick outhouse, and
the council
tear it down

You box
so hard
the slates
fall from the roofs
down
Walnut Street

You touched
my boyhood cheeks
with oil stained
hands: told
stories
on lie-in
Sunday mornings

You raged
with brute forearms
hammering out
steel casings

You held
your tongue

when I was
young, drunk
desperate

You forgave me
my art, my
raw
public posturing

You showed me
the edges
of Ireland:

      the

          crashing waves

      the

          mountains

      the

          passes

      the

          turf

      the

          stars
      the

          hounds, legends, secret places

          scent of Cuchulain

André Stitt

Substance

The boy would
wait and wave
each day
from beyond
a wall
outside
the city hospital

Covered in measles
shut out
of his mother's
presence, as
she lay in labour

Lying asleep
curled up
against
her pubic hair
against
the night
the demons.

In nineteen sixty-one
he flew to Paris
with his mother,
his brother, was
presented to
grandparents
threw up in the back
of an uncle's car

And down thru
all those years
she had kept it
that airline ticket
would take it out
look it over.

Ghost Dance

It's staggering
all over

     Manhattan

Faith grows
in moments
of exclusion

Dispatch a photo
Taken on Canal St.
when you

     were absent

stick it in a
bowl of rice

     Burn it, without
     your presence

watch it float away
watch it laughing

The grass grows
fierce and long

The sun bores
through everything

erases
     these memories

       eventually.

André Stitt

Warm Like The Sun, Strong Like The Ocean

I am sitting in an Ashton diner
looking out under the freeway
I am eating putines, and
she's standing on the other
side of the road, she
can't see me. I watch her
for a very long time, and
she looks lost in herself

I want to tell her it's ok, but
instead
I slump down inside
my plastic chair

I want to go out and hold her, and
tell her about my life, and
how I feel it all, how
I want to cry
for everyone.

Later, I am lying beside her
Laughing, and
I hold her belly close to mine
hold her in my strong arms
it's wet, the
smell of sex
is in the room

It's been raining
for a week now, and
she says
it's time to go
as she boards the coach
for Paris, and

I am trying to think
of tomorrow, when
it will be different, but
it's like a drug
I just love to get
fucked-up.

November Night, Oporto

Edge of world
basalt jetty roar
wing crash
Atlantic
steel bolt air

The edge of wisdom
                    fog mongrel dogs

at my heels,
guardian muzzle
                    weakened

limb legs
subtracted into
the funnel

                    into bottle

edge of mind
own end,
                    this heart

covered in tar
washed into venom

André Stitt

rain foam basalt

Dog end pier
sucked into trench
                plunge

tooth dog bone
                friend

my end, this night
                my home

The Man Whose Shoes Dissolved

Learn to play
with big sad
invisible wings

All angels navigate
your tired shoulders
eating their own lips

What do I know
we're all murderers

Splottlands

My heart and this life like
fishponds
and honeybats
hangs on all the jetplanes
that cross the mighty
horizon, the sunburnt lips
trees, buzzing satellites, and
the endurance of wisdom
that springs from the virtue
of no meaning that's delivered
from her brown eyed innocence
silver tongued style that
has kept us apart and from
being accountable
down here in Splottlands.

See me, I smoke
a big cigar, and
keep migrating, it
gets to be a habit
passing from land
to air, to land, as your
little ship, out there
on the ocean springs holes, and
you will never get to Cardiff, you say,
in a boat full of holes, though
my tears have swollen
your belly in a constant
shock of harassment, travelling,
held in detention, I will never
see your face again, and
this shame will be relived
over and over again
down here in Splottlands.

What I wonder will we all remember
at the end of our days, our life
once long ago, will it be a touch,
a laugh, a smile on a bus, that
still born child, the criminality
of love and garbage; I keep on travelling
sweating you out of every pore, and
chanting, chanting, chanting;
Fuck out the wonder
Fuck out the joy
Fuck out the talking
Fuck out the dreaming
Fuck out the meaning
down here
down here in Splottlands.

Lynne Rees

White

She tackled the flat first, painted walls and ceilings,
re-tiled the bathroom, laid a carpet – a thick
marshmallow pile that crept between her toes
and fingers. That prompted her
to remove the mauve from all her nails.
White would be her god from now.
She'd been through Designer Clothes,
Foreign Foods – she'd delivered monologues
on sushi – and then New Age.
Well, she had her own idea. An Original.
She'd be the one they talked about
in years to come. The one who started White.
She fitted high watt bulbs in every room,
bleached her hair and eyebrows platinum,
a double pack for maximum strength
and removed all other body hair.
But still she thought how positively dark
she looked in all this light, how much her hips
resembled pork against the marble bath.
She tried bathing according to the books
on purification, adding a capful of bleach
then five more, but the skin around her nails
began to peel. And even though
she'd drape herself in white from head to toe,
the colour of her hands and neck would interfere.
She began to hate the evening, the way
shadows insinuated through her room
and how the morning burst upon her
with its blue. She kept the halogen on

night and day and the curtains drawn.
White rice, white sugar, white bread. She loved
the translucency of reduced fat, skimmed milk
or Pernod poured on ice.
Since the bleach hadn't worked she took
to dusting baby powder on her face and lashes,
painting her lips with skiers' balm.
She dreamed of snow,
ran her hands along the ice walls
of her freezer, turning it to number six
so she could watch them grow, the meeting
of her breath with ice breath as she opened the lid.
She tried sitting in it and suddenly understood –
it wasn't her skin to blame. It was her blood.
She checked out all the clinics, got the best.
I want white blood she said at the desk.
The nurse just smiled, said *Sign here*
and *How will you be paying?*
How right she felt watching her blood
pump away to surplus stocks while she filled
with a master blend of glucose and salt.
Why hadn't she thought of this before?
After all, her bones were white. She knew
from the time she'd snapped her wrist,
the break so clean, so sharp, she'd seen
the ivory shear through her skin.
All those years of mistakes and fashion fads.
But this was The Look she was after.
She could see the magazine reports,
the glossy pictures – white leather,
alabaster walls, limed wood,
the bloodless silk of sheets absorbing
her barely perceptible frame.

The Snow Queen

Tough women always get bad press.
Cold. Bossy. Bitch. They said
I took him from the arms of his family
when he tagged along after me.

Ill-matched from the start
but I couldn't resist those young hands
on my skin. And though I've always been one for the cold,
a bracing walk, a bitter wind to blow a mood away,
I changed, spent days and nights sweating with him.

The week I went back to work,
I'd come home to find him buried under blankets,
the heating full on, his face as red as chestnuts,
not a scrap of housework done. Windows steamed
from his heat, his breath, his feet.
I slept in my own spare room

when I couldn't stand his body's furnace another night
while he spread hot and moist across my cool, white sheets.
The stench in the morning made me gag,
throw the windows open to his moans,
the condensation, the flowering of mould.
So don't tell me the old seduce the young.
He took me all the way.

The day I found him gone, I wept for joy,
for the cool setting on the shower,
the welcoming cold of the lavatory seat,
and then for fear of being alone. The bleak
expanse of mattress when I woke, a silence
that could decorate the walls.

It's months and I still miss the things
I grew to hate. Warm hands around my face.
At night, his heat rising against my spine.

Suddenly Awake

as if your heart's gone abseiling
or bungee jumping, or even if it might have
sneaked out to visit its neighbours –
the kidney sisters in their neat little identical houses,
or the slob of a liver who spends hours
oozing over a couch watching daytime soaps –
and not left you a note to explain its absence.

It returns of course, within seconds
hauling itself up and squeezing sideways
through the cage of your ribs
hoping it hasn't been missed
and, you hope, happy to be back, maybe
deciding to bake a chocolate cake, or relax
in a tub of bubbles with Barry or Julio
and their *Greatest Love Songs* CDs.

But there could be more to it.
It could be deliberately hiding
and holding its breath to show you
who's really in charge.

Cold

She likes the cold,
steps out of the house each morning
to feel the frost. When he calls her in
her hands are blue bones
translucent as skimmed milk.

At night she dreams of snow,
hers the only footsteps
puncturing the skin. She shivers
when they touch, when his breath, warm
breath trickles over her back.

Teaching a Chicken to Swim

Each Sunday she unwrapped a pimpled bird
from its cardboard tray and cling film,
cut away the string to free the headless body –
loosening wings and plump, bound hips –
and gently laid it in the bath. Sometimes
the water filled the yawning hole
or leaked between flesh and skin
and bubbled into blisters. She persevered,
couching the bird in open hands,
urging it to try, to slice the water
with its featherless, aerodynamic wings.
She needed the inert frame to pull away,
splaying those irregular fins
and march its cropped and wanting legs
along the length of bath, turning at each end
as neatly as a chicken on a spit. She needed
just one successful launch.

The Time-Stealer

I dread his step outside, his raincoat
always belted, hands fisted into pockets, eyes
searching through glass for time on my wrists

and shelves, the sweep of hands on watches,
alarms, old clocks – white faces trapped
inside a case of wood. Or at the kerb,

a shoulder tilted to my empty car,
waiting for the minutes to grow, his head
dipping to the blink of numbers, a slow

deliberate check. He is insatiable for it.
He will have me give it all to him.
He will have my heartbeats if I let him.

Moving On

From where I lie I can pick you up in an inch
of space between my thumb and finger, and put you
down anywhere – out onto the sea to bob along
in your metal framed, candy striped boat. Or here
next to me, so I can taste the salt on you.

Or along the beach among the sea cucumbers,
shrinking to millimetres as you travel. You're light
as the wind as I whisk you over the sand, and unaware
of your own fantastic journey – your muscles, limbs,
puppets to the pressure of my fingertips.

I can crush you, press gently until my thumb
and finger meet, squeeze all the sea water
out of you, rub the skin together until you're
just the grains of yourself. But I don't.
I return you to the place you chose, at the edge

of the sea, your back bent over and glowing
in the sun, liberating shards of seashells
from between your toes. I ease my fingers away
and your hand lifts, runs through your hair
as if missing the weight of something from above.

Ripe Fruit

While I am choosing beefsteak tomatoes in Good Earth,
I see her in the distance marching down Pacific Avenue,
bare breasts swinging. She is laughing. I look away,
concentrate on my hands – their own two pounds of ripe fruit.

She passes the split window of the grocery store. Her breasts
are huge, humungous icing bags of flesh slung from shoulders,

but brown from the sun. Her skirt is blue and long. Her open
shirt flares in the breeze rolling up Pacific from the sea.

There are police at the intersection. Will they stop her there?
Will she help them bundle her breasts back into the flimsy cotton
of her shirt? Will she resist them, or quietly watch as they fumble
with each one, embarrassed at the weight in their hands
threatening to break free from the rickety clutch of buttons?
Will she still be laughing or will she start to cry,
wondering why the morning had to come to this?

One Day the Wind Began to Blow and Didn't Stop

But it was fun – we laughed
at the twisting columns of leaves,
our neighbour's patio set blustering down the street,
ourselves leaning into it, how it knocked
the breath back into our lungs. We held each other
in the shelter of trees, planned to outrun it
hand in hand across a field. It didn't last.

We grew to hate the whip of it, car doors snapping
from our grasp, lips chapped, scalps gritty
with dust. We stayed in, arranged our lives
on the Web – money, books, food, wine -
got used to the way the house constantly creaked,
gave up filling cracks in the bedroom walls
and time-tabled our days to check the garden pots,
anchor them with stones.

Sometimes, when the weather warms up
we take off our clothes in the garden
and watch them tugged from our hands,

circling upwards like ragged birds of prey.
It nags at the small places on our bodies –
the creases at the corners of our mouths,
the tight plains at the backs of our knees.

We dream of boats mirrored on lakes.
We end our prayers with words of calm.
We ache for rain to fall vertically.

When we glance outside
and see someone fighting the thrust of it,
we mutter *Fool,* though our necks prickle
and stretch for a last glimpse, a coat
billowing like a sail, or a mouth
sealed to something like a smile.

Visitors

We know they are coming,
the note slipped under the door
warns us of the time, their desire
not to disturb. The footsteps begin

at eleven, their charted lines
of longitude and latitude leading them
to this pinhole on the map,
their hushed chatter as if
the last thing they want on earth
is to wake us.

By three they are pegging out the land,
small wooden stakes thumping into the ground
around our house. And before dawn
we creep downstairs to slide the bolts,
fasten the shutters, pull the curtains
tight. We even tape up the letterbox.

At first we can ignore them –
their laughter, the noisy way they eat,
the singing late into the night,
the occasional call for us
to come out and sit in the sun.
But by the end of the week

one of us will argue
we were hasty, from the start
there was nothing to be fearful of,
that we misread their intentions.
And one of us will sneak down
in the dark to unbolt the door.
One of us will be laughing
as the key turns in the lock.

Like Water

A tendon flickers in your wrist like an eel
then flits between the channel of bones,
the pulse at the side of your neck
checks your heart's tide of blood, breath
ripples in your sleeping throat, and this reminds me
how sometimes you are like a great wave
rushing me along the coast of your life,
and other times like the shadowed corner of a pool,
the weight of water unfathomable

but most of the time you are like one of those trick taps
suspended over a pond, seemingly unattached
to any supply, but the stream of water
constant, clear, flowing up as well as down,
and me wanting to believe in the magic,
that you can defy gravity, that not all tricks
are in the eye, the sleight of a hand.

Lorna Lloyd

The Cracked Lighthouse Prism

Dad's gift - big as a cartwheel
was wrapped in tarpaulin and
steered carefully down the pathway

Cutting rope knots, he left us to
peel back the dull green lid from
Apollo's cracked eye

A fierce white wink blinded us
then dunked our elastic heads
into a bright pool of bent sky

Aurora borealis crazied the paving
scribbled over the lawn
raced to bruise red bricks
and smear windows opalescent

Sparks electrified our vision
with a rash of floating stars

Burnt newspapers sent cinder words
flurrying across gardens
writing smut on flapping sheets

Scorched skin erupted in bubble blisters
singed hair shrank to a dolly's perm

Locust kids swarmed at our heels as we
rolled the sun down the road that hot afternoon
hurling rainbows into a cloudless sky -
burning everything in our path

Paris Taxidermist's Shop

A moose screams sideways in the foyer
Its rigid, lolloping tongue, chasing moss
Between teeth -missing since Piaf lived

Pea green walls sprout horns like
Hooks for enormous coats
A suspicious turtle with linoleum skin
Ushers customers inside a hushed zoo-permarket

Rotten floorboards tilt and creak
Threatening to flip over and tip
You onto the bloodied cellar table

Shelves of aged infants totter
Slither and gawp from death's pic n'mix
Sweeping overhead a mallard mobile
Hangs like a target for toddling royalty
In its shadow a cat licks its smile
So real I ask it a question it can't answer

A daft, dab of a mole backstrokes over
Resin bark, pink embryo hands, soft
As brushed nylon, paddling madly
Towards the millennium

Alloy beetles, neat as cars
Are parked alongside venomous queens
Pinned to red velvet like a tray of
Punk brooches precious under glass

Tied to a hat stand, a baby elephant's
Unravelling trunk, sniffs for its mother
Whose head crashes through plaster
In the outsize department

Frantic eyes search east, west
Her headless ghost haunting another continent

All the undead look through the living
In a timeless spell- waiting for a princess
To come and kiss the century old gorilla's
Horrifying lips - alive

Calendula

I harvested seed last autumn
Wintered them in darkness
In spring tiny fossils grew lime flesh
By June embryos became shaking hydra

Seed draws inward like clawed fists
You hid secrets that way - I had to guess
What treasures you held - the knot of a
Crushed spider, a GI Joe gun, nothing

The garden shrieks cadmium orange
Sparse petals lash upholstered eyes
Like the sunrays you drew - an infant
Piercing heaven with blazing spears

Today is your birthday - I grew a man
You strum soft notes on a new guitar
They follow my steps along the border
As I snip heads and rattle my bag

You keep time while I unpick
Folded minutes from imploded clocks
Each seed leaves an imprint in the husk
Like a dent on a cold pillow

Spiderman

You won't hear him scale your wall
He's too clever for that
Too perfect a hero
To disturb your sleep

Nor will you feel his velvet hands
Smooth and stroke you
As he ties you up in
Sticky silk threads

You will never guess the position
He stitched you on his web
Or remember the love song
He drummed for hours

Or how all his eyes
Searched your face
For pleasure, for pain
As his fangs pierced your breast

Tickling and running over your curves
Clinging and wriggling like water
Cocooning you so lovingly

And as daybreak performs her shadow play
He will unravel you slowly
Comb your hair and
Leave you dreaming

Of trussing up Peter Parker
The quiet man next door
Hungrily eating him for breakfast

Lorna Lloyd

Granny's Glass Eye

When I spoke to Granny
her one eye never listened;
half her face looked over my head
throughout the conversation.

Sucking a gobstopper once I choked;
spitting it free from my purple face
I knew it would be her glass eye.
Playing marbles I cried,
because the big one I aimed at
looked back at me.
A terrible gnawing wish
defeated any clear thought
to ask her to take it out
so I could stare into the hole it left behind.
I stood by her bedside,
waiting for her to wake,
wanting to open the white pot where it slept
and offer to push it gently in.

That unmoving eye was my only interest.
My eyes would fix upon its mystery
so I never listened to a word she said.
I had this nightmare of losing one of mine -
screaming in the blind night,
" Is my eye still there?"
It couldn't wink or follow,
echo love or dream. It was a fish-eye,
a dead eye of melted milk bottles.
I liked to play `Granny`- a ping-pong ball,
with a biro iris, floated in a margarine tub
on my bedside table.
They said Glaucoma took it.
Did he take a spoon and fish it out?

Did he suck it hard until it popped?
Did he swallow it?

I don't remember much about Granny but her glass eye
I wish she had left it to me in its white pot
so I could take it out, hold it in my palm
and make it look in my direction.

Fly Trap

Yawning bruised fruit promises,
she gargles flowerful juices and
teases with her pierced lips,
curled in a kitten snarl.

Black acrobats tiptoe through fish teeth,
slip and tickle down her tacky throat,
moonwalk into an acid green jacuzzi.

Zipped lips squeeze abdomens
that drip inside a body bag
fitfully zizzing electric distress.

Excitement bubbles as they
drown in sweet belly waves,
trapped inside a swollen purse,
where all sound, all flesh, dissolves.

Sucking on silence she hungers for
the frisson of insect percussion.

Unhinging clamped jaws
her gaping mouth cups
a wisp of torn wing.

Lorna Lloyd

Stargazers

A gift of lilies
creamy white pods
fragile as eggs, hung in the air

In a hot house of deceit they
unravelled frilled tongues
and breathed an odour so strong
they sexed the room

Lips on stalks
strained to kiss his passing hands
and smear him
with iodine powder
each stain - indelible as blood

All his past loves
sniggered from the vase

But I kept their slender
stems too long
left them standing
in foul water

Falling mouths
bloomed like rust
on cut glass

At night I moisturised
with plant extracts and
watched my reflection
outgrow the mirror

Every part of me swelling
while those Stargazers
disrobed, unobserved
in the dark

Frida Kahlo's Itch

This itch is getting worse
and the plaster cast smells bad

I've painted every inch I can reach
my bed is a gallery
and I'm a masterpiece

a turtle flipped belly-up
a sterile mummy
a broken compass

but describing myself has become boring
as picking at my edges

I miss my monkey and Diego
they said the monkey was missing me
they didn't mention Diego

In my sleep I was running home
to the blue house
opening my chest like swing doors

I smashed the embryo's glass
and planted the ochre child right here
where my belly button must be pooled in sweat
my baby grew through me like a vine

Cicadas sound like scratches don't they?
could you drop one inside my carapace?
so that its wings fret
in my confined spaces
and its filthy nails
scrape a route out
through me

Lorna Lloyd

Puddles

You know the way a puddle reflects the universe
Inviting you to leap into heaven
That's him
Pretending to be deep
When an inch down I hit rock bottom

You know the way an onion looks
All that golden varnished skin
That's him
Unpeeling his clothes
Disappointment makes me cry

You know the way a Lighthouse shines
That's him
Illuminating my life when turned on
But then it's two in the morning
Pitch black, and I don`t know when, if, he'll be back

You know the way a poem
Sometimes makes an absurd connection
That's him
Lyrically professing his affection
When I know he borrowed every word

Tiffany Atkinson

Adult Thinking

Take, for example, this beach: more a stretch of pigskin
swabbed with flies, and scarcely the place to savour your
                                        icecream
or chips, much less knuckle down with a lover, less still
to bring your kids; the sea a disc of hammered tin
with a corpsy tang and rusting, lethal edge; but the truth is
it's late, there's an ache putting root in your back's groove,
and with no-one to tell you better, you barely care
that the flies don't know you from carrion, not when this
                                        rock here
has just the curve to fit your spine so your upturned face
gets a widescreen gape of sky, and if the sun were to come
                                        round,
well, you'd be there for the taking; so it strikes you,
as you spark up one of the cigarettes you quit last week,
that you're settling for less these days; that, at the same time,
there are worse, no, infinitely worse things.

Paddling

My grandmother stands on the sea's lip,
a weathered Aphrodite
in an oyster-coloured mac.
Beyond her the egoless blue
flickers with sails.

My father and I hang back.
We expected Sunday clothes,
a sheer drop to a grievous sea,
a scattering as of confetti. Instead

241

she shucks her shoes and popsocks
and I glimpse her feet for the first time:
pale Victoriana on the packed sand.

It's early March. The water
bites her ankles as she wades
through bladderwrack and flotsam,
lifting her hem above the breathing swell.
She casts his dust on the webbed foam,
watches the teak box fill and sink.
Gulls work the sky like scissors.
A day made for sailing, and his dinghy
gone for a song to a London couple
with three kids and a hatchback.

She turns, and the low sun
strikes her eyes' flint.
There are traces of what might be ash
on her damp shins, but we say nothing.

Babysitter

So you count out an hour
in five-minute segments of pizza
till her cry beats in semibreves
down two flights.
You carry her out like salvage,
barefoot over sheer floors
to the kitchen's chill. Against
your denimed hip she's all surface
and roll, a live weight, light packed
into her in fistfuls. She brims and kicks
while you fumble with formula, teaspoons, Calpol—
she's the expert here, and knows it.
Down through a decade's empty rooms
your mother's disappointment
falls in crisp pleats.

Stroke

So I drive for the first time this season,
grinding gears like a bonesetter
through two counties, keeping
a headful of place-names, popsongs,
advertising jingles, anything.

You're half-in, half-out
and spare as a zen parable.
Your tongue lifts like gold-leaf
when I lean in to decipher.
Old seducer, your eyes knit light

to the same, cruel, Saxon blue. Yes
I know you, walking without help
like a dowser, astonished by your own feet.
You've no mind for the practical,
but it won't wait. I'll be clearing

the cottage as-soon-as, wearing
the plaid shirt you kept for the roses,
dosing myself with the brandy, which
you'll not miss. I'll be every bit as ruthless.
Your neighbours are sheer concern,

warning that the half-read book,
the teacup, the biscuit missing a bite
are hardly a job for a woman in my state.
Their sprung smiles bay for a lick
of the old hurt, but I won't have it.

Taxi Driver, September 2001

Outside the cinema
you put on American rage

and hardly expect it to fit like buckskin
or give you a whiff of distant slaughter,

only now I'm walking home with Travis Bickle,
high on the kick of weaponry

cocked in his body's oiled sockets,
staring his own reflection out in shopfront glass

while I flutter like Betsy in my chilly
origami frock. But it's little, ribby Iris,

wide-eyed, stoned as the woman taken,
sizing you up from under her floppy-brimmed

hat, that gets you most. Now you take aim
from the foot of the bed, rehearsing the things

a 44 magnum can do to a woman's face,
and worse. You're joking, of course,

but then, that's muzzle at my throat,
and baby, you I'm looking at.

Tea

You made me tea
while I shook the rain from my jacket.
You stooped to fit into the kitchen,
but handled the cups as if they'd been
the fontanelles of two young sons
whose picture sits in the hip of your 501s.
We spoke of – what? Not much.

You weren't to know how your touch
with the teaspoon stirred me,
how the tendons of your wide, divining hands
put me in mind of flight.

You wouldn't have known
when you bent to tend a plant
that your shirt fell open a smile's breadth.
You parted the leaves and plucked
a tiny green bud. Best to do that
with the early ones, you said.
I thought of the salt in the crook
of your arm where a fine vein kicks.
Of what it might be like to know
the knot and grain and beat of you;
the squeak of your heart's pips.

Testimonial: Iscariot

Fathers, elders, only
consider it this way. The act so mortally simple,
a child's task. His cheek as warm bread; a touch of salt
about his mouth, a delicate scratch of herb. My palm
against his clean breast. Caught between the taking-leave
and having done, a fraction ahead of the tiny event
no merciful g-d would allow. Believe, there was faith
on my tongue, through all the hours the lamps were bright,
the doors ajar, while meat and wine passed hand to hand
that final Pesach night. He was morbid, subdued. We
all thought it due to the wine, knowing him to be untouchable:
through him slipped miracles. But, fathers, elders,
let it be said how he knew, even then, it was as good as done;
and of flood, or bolt, or burning bush, came none.

Umami

Take strawberries: a deep, hearty bowlful
you should have picked yourself. Wipe and hull
and quarter, one by one. Drop in a bain-marie
with an inkling of sugar, and leave them
to express themselves. They will hang
in muslin overnight, giving up a slow pulse.

Now bring wine to the boil's brink.
Flame it to draw the acid's splinter. And
distil the whole lot down with citrus pulp
to a mellow pool. Be prodigal with pepper
and quicken with vinegar. The briefest glint
of chilli, shot of orange flower water. You

are aiming past salt, sweet, sour, bitter, for
umami, the elusive fifth sense. Mouth-feel,
shimmy of molecules over the tongue's bulbs,
riff through the nasal caves. Bloom of crimson
glimpsed at the corner of the palate's eye,
a late wave breaking low in the throat.

Plain bowls are best. The squeak of white
against that ribald red. Anoint each meniscus
with a glam of olive oil. Cast rose petals over.
This is not to be served up lightly. Come
to the table with a clean slate, warm from a day
lived well-enough through, mouth in full spate.

Photo from Belfast

I knew him, the dead boy, Michael.
Only for three hours, maybe, taken in all.
He stopped me for a light outside my local—
I fell for the accent, the smile. I'd no particular errand
that August Saturday, and stood him a pint.
It was one of those conversations you have perhaps
twice in your life; in full-flash, polaroid.
I was the one took his picture on the Queen's Road,
after he took mine. We were both half-cut by then.
The car was a chunk of dark, behind and to his right.
Blue, maybe black, dead shiny. I'd a new pair of jeans on
and clocked my shape in its panels on the way in.

I'd have stayed for the fourth pint, only
I was mulling over a pair of spike-heels I'd taken
a shine to a while back. Truth is,
when the car put a root of white heat through the tarmac,
made light of the pub, and punched out the street
in a riptide of splinters, I was three blocks east
with his number tucked in my backside pocket
and my heart set on a pair of fuck-me shoes;

and that has a way of shifting your focus,
making you rethink your image. Since I heard
they'd turned up his camera, since I saw the footage
I've been framing everything in split-seconds;
shutter-speeds, degrees of exposure. I develop him
nightly from the reeling dark – each particular fluke
of space, time matter. You'd not think it difficult,
to filter him down through the pinhole of morning,
to bring him back to light, to get the picture.

Tiffany Atkinson

The Anatomy Lesson of Dr Nicolaes Tulp, 1632

Hung for thieving a coat in the raw new year
Adriaenszoon lies on the slab for Dr Tulp,
who takes the stage in sweeping gallows black
as the good guildsmen of Amsterdam flock round
in a quackery. This Tulp has a feeling for light
and shade. Behold how he unpicks the knot
of the offender's left hand, the insinuating scalpel
paring back skin like the peplum of a tulip. Such
immaculate work: the smooth-cheeked spectators
press in, anaesthetized by high, white ruffs, purveyors
of tendon and carpal. With watchmaker's nicety,
Tulp applies forceps to the *flexorum digitorum,*
and the dead man's hand becomes fist. All is decorum
as the deadpan Doctor makes a case of Adriaenszoon.
The gentlemen, for the most part, keep their corruption
at arm's length. Tulp's in up to the neck. Between them
they'll have two coats off the poor man's back.

Tôpher Mills

Apron

My Mother had a string of men
who phoned her days and evenings.
They'd ask briefly after my father, Ken,
who was never in, and then
they'd want to know what she was cooking.
She'd tell them in great detail, explaining
the recipes, why the ingredients,
what they did, how to concoct them.
She could whip up, ad hoc, in fun,
something on the spot, her instincts
for the delicious absolute, unwavering.
A platinum blonde of the kitchen
she'd tell them what it looked like
how it tasted, the texture, what it went with,
and these men, whose wives could barely open
packet mash, hung on every word, lingering
ear sweat-sealed to the receiver, salivating.

T.B.

I am blowing up my father's left lung.
It is huge and covered in old TB scars.
I cannot hyperventilate fast enough
the hole in it burbles deflatingly.
I've got to keep puffing harder and harder
until the doctors can invent micro-surgery.

* * *　* * *　* * *

In the 1950's TB ward they had enormous pills
that tasted so bad the only way to eat them
was plopped into the morning's sugary porridge.

My father and his fellow patients
are hanging from the top of a door
pulling themselves up to see over it
the man who eats the pills raw
chews them and their papery wrappers
with a relished grim determination.

The other patients go out at weekends
get plastered so bad it counteracts
any good they do being in hospital.
My father is up in the morning
running around the grounds of Sully
in his dressing gown and slippers
keeping fit for his eight hour shifts.

* * *　* * *　* * *

They want to put their eye down his throat
but my father won't let them.
He wants to go home where he's safe,
where he knows he'll be okay.
"They've seen enough of my bloody innerds
and I've seen enough of them!"
My mother has started to pray again.

The Modern Poet's Fetish for a Map Poem

Philip's Mercantile Marine
Atlas of the World, 1904.
He opens it at the equator
huge pages, card-thick,
their edges worn soft and floury.
Charting oceans with equal importance
to the multi-coloured lands

it would have been splayed
on the bridge of some ship
loaded with phosphorous
nudging small icebergs
through the Magellan Strait.

He rips the pages out carefully
lays them flat, 20 by 30 inches,
the seven seas across his floor.
Placing his body patterns over them
his West German scissors start to cut
and all the cartography bends and shifts,
tectonic plates cavorting
into a warped, unknown planet.

Folding and sewing he joins new worlds.
Pacific and Atlantic back to back,
the coasts of China and Japan merging
with Europe, Scandinavia and Russia.
His feet become icy Poles apart,
the Americas span his mid-drift,
Australia a skewwiff corkless hat,
Africa and India his sturdy legs.
On a whim he uses the leftover U.K.
for a big knotted wide-boy tie.

Adorned, his map fits well.
So enchanted to be charted
he wishes to show off his new found
man of the worldliness.

At the local pub, wearing geography,
his Earth carouses in like the wind,
shimmers in a Black sea of liquor,
Karaoke's the scorched wildernesses
till he ruffles out, a looming storm cloud
to the nearest disco's mirrored globe
below which his paper planet will twirl.

Hat floating off the sweaty edge,
his latitude gyrating longitude,
his jacket full of hurricanes,
his trousers full of tidal waves
till his torrential drinking
drains the Dead Sea and his poles
global warm him to the street
where earthquakes shift his axis,
he head butts the man in the moon
and his orbit collides with the gutter.
There his molten stomach erupts
and his tie suffers devolution.

He lays moaning like the Himalayas.
Jacket and trousers totally tornadoed
their continents awaiting the ridge
of low pressure from the North
whose rain will gently
wash him mapless.

Dis is jest tuh say like
(translated from William Carlos Williams)

Dat I skoffed
duh sarnee
yoo id in
duh freezuh kumpaartmunt

an wat
yooz wuz praps
kraabin
fuh laytuh like

Sorree yuhno
ir wuz jaamtastik
reelee baabaaaneree
an reelee baaraaas

Nevuh Fuhget Yuh Kaairdiff

Fraank Fanaarkaapaanz on duh mitch
inis bestest daps
onis faastest underaang bogey
like uh propuh Beano comic

Mad Motters donkeyin
raaysin froo Grange-end gaardns
korzin uh woppin grate malaarkey
dodgin duh diddykoys

scraamblin kross duh daaffs
kraakin jelly froo duh chewlips
an nuh Paarkeyz frowin uh wobbley
totulley owta duh winda like

"BLUDDY LIDDUL DOWZOWS"
ee yelz all jottld up to is nodgem
"YEWUL GET SUM GROLLUP YEW ERVA
PAARKS YUR AARS ROWUND YUR AGEN"

Motter mite be beejobulld
buh Fanaakaapaan ees norra dill
iss is dreem wen ee growz up
tuh bee obbuldeeoy tuh duh kween

aan duh Paarkeyz aad uh maajorum
is germojumz gon all maankey
"Faaraawaakin bolluhwoks" ee baars
"iyum orf down duh skin ows"

aark aark duh laark
frum Kaairdiff aarms paark
iyull aav uh Klaarksee pi
aan un aarf aan aarf uh Daark
aa aan
uh baanaanuh jaam saarnwidj

The Last Swim in Empire

Today he has swum the last big 50.
He has the pleasant, tired looseness
the after swim ease of everything
as if he were still in water
floating through the blue
gently covered in coolness
as the gliding plash of the overarm
noses into the whispering rush.
The regulars had parted affirming
'Last day in the old pool, first day in the new.'
with all the mock certitude of a large rock

slumbering down to a murky ocean floor.
From that downward wending escapes
the minute bubble that is Wales.
How long will it take to emerge
in a splutter of unintelligible linguistics
as its air becomes everywhere else.

Perhaps his thirty years of afternoon swims
will return him to play in Cardiff's bay,
all silted, choked and barraged, where
as a child he laughed through ships wakes
with a pat of butter hidden under a flat stone
to rub off black oil stains from wet skins.
Now, being much more accomplished in water,
he'll swim out through the Bristol Channel,
into the Irish Sea and, oblivious of the pollution,
will slap every wave with the energy
of the new born enthusiast.
Carousing with dolphins,
splashing curious seagulls
and shadow boxing nervous sharks,
water rapturously gurgles beneath
as his body reaches for movement and air.
The sensual mile or so of depth below
just a breath of mist on the earth's mirror.
With all tiredness hours away,
the challenge of an unused body
between the bright blue and the dark green,
a speck sandwiched by two atmospheres,
he knows, like all the creatures,
languages and cultures of the sea,
the land, the air and beyond
to strange planets and stranger oceans,
that to swim is everything.

Tôpher Mills

Lavernock Point

Looking for somewhere to do it
they come across another couple doing it.
Too embarrassed to pass by they shuffle back
to walk in a wide arc from the rocks
to the strands of sand and shale at the sea's edge.

They glance enviously, a hundred yards away,
at the undulating, heat-hazed couple.
His white buttocks thumping, head bobbing,
her brown hands clawing and
her light soles a halo of activity.

Out of view and back at the warm rocks
her cut off shorts prove momentarily awkward
and the towel doesn't take the roughness
from the spreed of barnacles as they'd hoped,
but how delicious the cool, gentle sea-breeze
caressing the hot crack of his arse,
coaxing out her whiskery nipples.

After climaxing in a froth of saltiness
they sit up to see the other couple
walking at the sea's edge, trying to look away.
They laugh raucously and drain the last
of the Californian pink white wine.

They have yet to get bitten by the sandflies
or spot the large sweating man up on the cliffs
crouching behind his camcorder.

Ifor Thomas

My recurring nightmare is trigonometry

Once again I am sitting at a small desk
the single unblinking eye of a blank inkwell,
old wood as hard and polished as stone
cratered with carving, unknown initials.

My pens and pencils, a rubber, set square
are marshalled like troops deployed to the wrong front.
The examination paper is virgin snow,
tracked only by wild animals.

An invigilator patrols the varnished straits
the breath of his gown on my cheek
heels clicking, out of time with the clock
whose ornate hands do not move.

Exam panic grips my throat, sweats my hand -
why am I doing the trigonometry paper?

I am fifty-two,
I own my house, car
my children are gone
I run my business
my marriage is secure.

But still the trigonometry question demands an answer.

Llawhaden: 19 May 2000

Edith Thomas, 91, lies lost in the rubble
of C16 Llawhaden House. She has stumbled
once too often, this time into the two bar electric fire
and her nightie has turned her into a roman candle.

Johnny Owen, 89, the last man to see her alive,
after 68 years now unemployed, says, "she was a real lady."
PC Cowper, 25, drapes the scene-of-crime tape.
He is a police officer destined for a good career.

Opposite Llawhaden House is Llawhaden Castle
built by Bernard, the first Norman bishop of St. David's.
Llawhaden straddles the Landsker, both English and Welsh
were once spoken here. The fire fighters all speak English.

My mother, 85, fluently bilingual, fiercely Welsh
peers through the Herris fencing for an interesting cutting
opts instead for a 2 inch screw dropped by the builder
who erected the DANGER DO NOT ENTER sign.

This visit pleases my mother, scathing as she is of old
                              women who live alone,
drowning in their baths, burning down their mansions,
going ga-ga without style or presence of mind
while she sails on serenely.

What to say when criticising poetry
(like this poem)

The title's good
>   (I can't think of anything to say about this poem)

Can you read it again?
>   (give me time please to think of something to say)

It's too long
>   (never it's too short)

Lose the last line
>   (and the rest of it for all I care)

The idea behind the poem is better than the poem itself
>   (although that's not saying much)

I like your new approach to language
>   (are you dyslexic?)

Some of your images are truly memorable
>   (whose poem have you ripped off?)

Isn't this two poems in one?
>   (it's a mish mash)

I need to read this on the page
>   (It's too dense, like the poet)

You read your poetry really well
>   (but you write like an arsehole)

Have you thought about your audience?
>   (this poem is therapy - see a psychiatrist)

You could place this somewhere
>   (like the bin)

It's a new approach to an old theme
>   (it's a clichéd mess)

It's a good performance piece
>   (it's crap.)

Have you thought about putting the last line first?
>   (like this poem)

When your wife suspects you of having an affair

She will wait until you have entered the kitchen
before sniffing the air, and touching your shoulder
as if you were stuffed with horsehair.

She will stare into your eyes, for the image of a lover
will be imprinted there, then ask:
What was the weather at three this afternoon?

She will inspect your car with a magnifying glass
dust the dash for fingerprints, look for lint,
dirt or sand. There will be questions to answer.

She will check mileage, tyre pressures;
the angle of inclination of the seat,
then raise the bonnet, drain oil.

She will take your mobile phone
break it under the heel of her boot,
sift the fragments for strange numbers.

She will open a vein to take blood samples,
analyse your stomach contents
to check for fish, rich food and mangoes.

She will cut through your scrotum while you sleep,
dissect your vas to uncover recent sperm movements,
explore further, touch the prostrate - find it stiffening.

She will lie next to you,
wait for your lips to mutter another's name,
watch your eyelids flicker in your nightmare.

She will cleave your skull with an axe,
dip her fingers into the images that fall out of
your optic nerve, is the brain still hot?

Then at the weekend you will have a smoke,
share a bottle of wine and she will laugh
as you tell her somebody else's joke.

Post Christmas Drink

How was Christmas for you?
I ask the barman
waiting for a Guinness to settle.

Christ I nearly died
woke up Christmas eve could hardly breathe
rushed into hospital left lung collapsed
never happened before, no warning
gave me drugs, had to pump it up
spent three days in intensive care
now here I am second day of the New Year
working like a dog.

He applies the finishing touches,
traces a lucky four leaf clover in the froth.
Have one for yourself, I say.

Going to see Lou Reed

She said
I'm going to see Lou Reed.
I said really, where?
She said here, in town.
I said is he still alive?
Walking on the wild side
with Warhol, Nico, Cale
and those.
Did any of them survive the sixties?
If they did, they shouldn't have.
People don't know when to stop
when to call it a day
when it's out of time
all blown out
finished
run dry
finis
kaput.

Still for old time's sake
I'll come.
She said
You'll be there anyway.
I said I will?
She said
I said I was going to see you read.
I said me? Read with Lou Reed?
She said forget it.
I think I'll stay at home
and listen to a record.

Doors

How can I forget these doors made of mahogany
on trestles, and me, the apprentice, sanding
every square inch? Gideon Delahay, craftsman,
joiner, with his kettle of warm water, approaches
through the rushing noise of the machine shop.
Mahogany is deceitful, the grain can run both ways.
He doesn't say much, Delahay, watches with
those narrow eyes, his face cut in half by
the shadow of the pulled peak of his flat cap.
As he tips the kettle, drops of water fall from
the burnt metal, catch the light, mercury in the dust.
Water raises the texture of this wood like
a hand running up the fur of a cat's back.
I pick up my sanding block, get to work
this time coming from the other direction.

Drag and push, drag and push
I hear this noise in the night
as my father sucks mustard gas in the trench
of his dreams. Sweat tracks my labourer's makeup
and hardwood dust burns my lungs.
This is the last job I will do on the tools
I watch Gideon Delahay hang the doors
in the façade of the Bute Street bank,
close them easy as if they ran on ball bearings.

I walked through them only yesterday.
There was a twinge of kinetic memory in
my biceps as I touched the iron surface.
It was that or arthritis. One world war,
two marriages, a heart attack, eighty years.
Pain visits the darkness of my body like meteors.

They are standing straighter than me, these doors.

Blocking signals to the heart

Timothy McVeigh's last meal was
two pints of mint choc chip ice cream.
Out of character this, if as reported,
he had adopted a strict vegan diet
to encourage the gaunt look of a martyr.
Still he keeps us guessing.
There is a small delay in the execution chamber –
problems with the live CCTV feed to Oklahoma.
The ten media representatives are patient
(as well they may be – this is a once-in-a-career
opportunity)

Sodium pentathol is an anaesthetic
It stops the brain reacting to nervous impulses

He keeps his eyes open – they all agree on this
but does he lift his head from the gurney
to stare defiantly at those who stare at him?
Not certain. The IV was already fixed to his right thigh
ready to deliver the three chemical cocktail.
A sheet covers his body and is folded over his chest
we must see his face as he dies
(unusual this, in most pornographic movies
the face is the last thing we want to see)
The IV line jumps as the chemicals flow.

Pancuronium bromide, is related to curare,
It paralyses the breathing muscles

He is now staring at the camera in the ceiling,
(our eye witness has it that he does not blink)
He takes puffs of air "as if fighting unconsciousness"
(– so he is defiant!)

After four minutes his eyes
glaze over, roll up slightly,
his skin turns yellow
his lips tinged blue.

Potassium chloride blocks electrical signals to the heart

He made his bomb of fertilser and fuel.
It killed 168 people.

Kiss

I knew something was wrong
when I kissed you that afternoon,
not the coldness of your forehead – we all get cold
nor its smoothness – you skin was always good.

It was, I think, the fact that you let me kiss you at all
you always turned away from such shows of affection

Death has certainly changed you.

Weather Forecast

Patterson has settled himself into my office.
His voice is like the weather forecast.
It drones on and by the time he's finished
I don't know whether it's going to rain in Wales
because I stopped listening around the Midlands.
The wind rattles a blind:
"Do you agree that's the best way forward?"
"Yes, yes, of course" I say.
He shuts the window and I open
an umbrella in my mind.

Alexandra Duce-Mills

another guildhall

a long thick-woven sack, pulled tight at the neck by a
                                                    length
of chain, the heavy-weight of wooden placards inside,
                                                    dragged
and lifted through town,

a struggle, operating alone, and noticeable,

for selling newspapers to indifferent shoppers

i am diarised,

i return to an empty house, knives and stones
rattling against the ribs,

i am ill,

there's pleurisy and pneumonia in hurricane charlie

i prolong my sickness

with cigarettes, it makes no difference,

i am detailed,

there is luxury in an empty house's quiet,

i take a bath, change into the woollen dressing gown that is
not mine, as scratchy as hessian,

the phone rings in the hall, a man called colin asks, is
                                                    andy in?

i know its them,

within twenty minutes, they arrive

i go through the kitchen doorway, and catch sight, they
don't see me, i'm hiding
flat to the wall, in the corner,

this is a real-life movie in the making,

the hammering at the back door, hammer hammer
                                        hammer,
louder than anything, louder than thunder on your
                                        doorstep,

they're uniformed, a van full,

they wear fluorescent jackets,

one climbs up onto the kitchen window ledge, another
opens the privy door he pisses all over, the floor, the walls,

i creep under the covers, *they'll find me like this*

i will be detained,

i will be denied a solicitor,

the knives in my chest cutting in, sweat-hot

turns cold,

i must've stayed there, under blankets pulled tight to my
                                        ears,

an hour at least,

the commandos leave empty-handed,

it takes a week or so, before i make the decision,

one evening,

leave everyone

debating as usual, amongst themselves,

safe in the safe house,

i close the bedroom door and sneak out without word,

cadre name cadre name comrades,

we dropped our rubbish in black bags from the fourth
floor,

we sat around trestle tables into the night,

they held a girl under, *where are the documents,
give us the documents!*

we jacuzzied in the nude,

we lied, we cheated, we stole
from penguin-suited theatregoers,

we were petitioners,

cop cars cruising slowly by, *i know you, i recognise your
face,*

we were lobbyists,

we were harbourers,

and now how indifferent, how ambivalent am i,

fifteen years on

now every minute isn't detailed, it isn't pencilled in,

or ....?

another guild hall,

no-one chants *whaddowewan whendwewannit NOW,*

no-one chants, even

silent committee rooms moccasin

sad harlequin socks,

marble cubicles pelmet *council members only,*

a secret gone rancid, by now

its an acid smirch,

the director of services raises

eyebrow issues, and they grip in,

hot calculator fangs,

in air

thicker for his wake, the red face

of his cleansed moustache,

to breathe him in is what they want,

but,

i could've made a stand,

on art-deco tables,

could've danced

a grand-piano-tango,

could have set

alight velvet, ...and meant it?

Alexandra Duce-Mills

electric sparks are bright orange fireflies

stay until the night draws dark in the taint of wood oil and
                                                         stains
on the concrete

sawdust vice-grips

machine tools hot burner gas jet still hot

a wooden handmade pair of ladders a metal lampshade swinging
made from a pudding dish swinging light shadow light shadow

a meat-safe put to new use and painted over this is what we used
to use before we had a fridge

purply-blue blood blisters welling black under the thumbnails band-
saw countersink different weights and gradients
can't get a purchase hold that end still if you can
pass the bradawl three eighths

circular saw three-ply
mark with a pencil across and down here
drawing a line with little finger as the guider
you can sweep up the sawdust but
oil will always stick to the brush

a metal industrial dustpan is heavy and solid

knock on the wall with a sanding block five times
and get the
answer two

avoid the full bag of cement it burns

this is a kingdom for the father and his two loyal

daughters
no-one else may pass

mitre the corners

hold steady

paper boxes are houses for nails and screws
in strong brown paper bags jack and jill

metal splinters hurt more

in a soft worn leather pouch there's a piece of magic shrapnel

glasspaper sandpaper linseed soaking in

the sort of question that should be asked of a son not the
youngest daughter

you know the scene in a film the father giving the boy cigarettes
over and over till he chokes and wants no more
i thought for a minute it was going to be like that
you want a packet of cigarettes yes i said

breath stemmed as father took a tin off the shelf
four squares of aluminium he'd seamed together with
solder

-sealed verona 1941- an inscription scratched in

so no promises were made of any kind
between us that afternoon

and ten years pass until the seal is broken one drunken evening
a knife is taken to it

someone who should be nameless

made the first stab

and there, ten victory v untipped cigarettes square they were
perfect in a soft paper packet

i swear never to...

they are placed in a plastic bag with a plastic seal hidden away
in a keepsake box

in only a few years the stalker compares notes with the rapist
and the husband spits until his mouth is dry

and then alone without anything in the back sitting room
here
a permanent blanket of smoke comforts

i light up the first chocolate tar blue *victory v*
fifty years in the vintage

the sorting-house

i will hold you as precious as a clutch
of four eggs, balanced between five fingers, when
you get old,

i'm soaking my feet in the open window's fan-light,
tapping at the wall, i'm directed
by the ceiling, ticking, clicking, shifting,

i am not able to help my self, so tempted,
i hold them up to the light, look for innards,
check if the germ's fertilised,

this hatchery is wicked, or could be,
a knitting needle pushed through the back
of the mother's armchair
whilst she sits, watching television,

i will try to think no further,
but if the curd and the seed of an idea is lying,
curled in there, forgotten,

rotting, stinking, and nobody knows it,
i'll scratch skin red, concentrate on distemper,
on shadows and cobwebs,

pressed awkward against rough plaster,
picking, looking, checking, fussing, clucking, touching,
in the darkening sorting-house,
water drip-dripping off the weeds on the waterwheel,
second, counted second,

can i put my thoughts away in there?
can i leave you in there, settled, nestled, precious,
that you may ne ver grow old?

let me always rest my sore ear against
the daddy-fabric
of your work suit,
and tell, tell, tell,
a feather's breath between us?

Annabelle Mooney

Sleep falls like water

I
The size of a bed is relative to its use.
It fits its groove.

II
We shape our bodies to the bed
You think that's wrong
But I've seen the way you move
When you think no one is watching
When you're not thinking at all
I've seen the looks that rise from your face.

I sleep sideways, curled in,
the square of body back and wall
making a safe rectangle.
My heart beats into the mattress.

III
I can sharpen sheets,
hospital corner sharp,
dog-eared pages
lying in piles of tissues
at my side, bottles overturned,
candles burning skin
into large yellow blisters.

IV
We sleep our beds to dream

V

I have tried to dream a future,
make it happen with pure force of image.
I have shaped sand into glass vessels
and poured into them,
I have made milk with my hands
and washed myself clean with it.

VI

I remember dreams
And have to drag myself up in the morning
I cry from yawning
My mouth opening in cyclops circle

If there is no dream there is no sleep
continuity of slippage;
to know that there is a before during and after.

VII

I don't know about travelling in sleep.
I don't know about leaving bodies
and moving huge distances.
But I have met people in the cross over
between;
when I am falling and they are rising.

I have met them as they were
crossing London Bridge,
undoing ourselves again.
I don't stop, talk,
but to know that there could
be a glance,
with a hand wiping sleep
or day from eyes.

This is something I think.

VIII
I have walked days
not knowing if one foot
would go in front of the other.
I have felt things that
the world tells me do not exist.

IX
Sometimes real damage is done on mattresses.
They are silent
Do not give explanations
though the evidence can be real.

I have woken with bruises all over my face
and marks on my legs
in places that only a mirror can reach.
I have woken with pains in my chest
that are not internal.
I have woken having been run over heavily.
I have woken with puffy eyes,
stung in the back.
My waist is a wasp
and it hums through to morning.

X
I have been dumped by waves
and dreamed of shores.
I have been dumped by water,
picked up and shaken
till I thought I would die,
the air pressed out of my chest
and trying to find the way out.
Water, soft.
I have been dumped by men,
dumped and bleeding.
Waves of them.

And yet I take them to my bed
to see how they sleep.
To watch them
and chart their patterns,
the isobars and topography
of their bodies at rest.
Sometimes they float and
sometimes they sink and
I don't know which is worse.
The celluloid snores, like bears
make my eyebrows twitch.
I have to move far away.
But I cannot find the next room.

XI
There is taste in dreams and touch.
I have tasted my own throat
cut from ear to ear.
Had the after ringing of death
in my ears for hours.
Have seen you wrestle and write
at four o'clock in the morning,
when I knew we were both asleep.
I have seen you move things around me.

XII
There are changes in sleep,
that last.
A look can be placed on your face
that you cannot erase.
I can see your guilty teeth
and your sharp grin so very high up.
Sometimes I feel your hands on me
the whole of the next day
and I have slept alone.

XIII
Sometimes I dream truth
and can't remember a single word.

Annabelle Mooney

The Pattern (with apologies to Vita Anderson)

When you are not here
I don't think of you at all

I don't think of you
When braiding my hair
I don't think of you
When I'm riding the bus
Or I'm polishing shoes
Or making gravy
When I'm tearing nails from my fingers
Or lighting the cigarettes you hate
Even when I'm thinking about you
I don't think of you

The hours in which I find you
Are yours

But
I wonder
if you imagine
I exist for you

I breathe only when you need me to
I move my body
Only in the way you want me to

But perhaps that's the way you like it

They are your words making me
Not my words speaking

Onion

You are in the garden in gloves, brown and rough.
With cigarette I fear for twigs and wrists
which may or may not
because of age
be in flames.

I sit, fish eyes taking in strange curves
at the edge of sight.
There is a sheet of light between us,
like glass and dust mixed thin.

I said to you,
I wish for the moon,
Finally, your elbows steeped in earth,
you walk towards me,
taking in the grass and the machinery
which has been left behind.
You are clicking to yourself
and sketching a map of time.
With you you carry a white clock,
faceless,
swinging in the air.

(The chair is to keep me
on the ground, not from it)

Your face curves as you climb
the steps towards me.
Your hands move apart,
a triangle of green forms suspended.
The moon, you say
and tie the green threads
you have dug woven,
around my neck.
In half covered tones
you breathe into my ear-
I know –

Annabelle Mooney

Untitled Poems

*

I can read backwards

Reverse printed
Negatives

I can blend into blank spaces.
A streetlight raises the veins on a leaf and I smile.

The light is not the same everywhere.
It moves like hands

I've left home before
And I can compose straight faces
Even close up
Even when you can see spaces in pupils
When something isn't right
When it needs touching up

Push it and feel.
It is done with light and mirrors.

He takes my hand and the shutter flexes.
Metal is not as straight edged.
His fingers find their space where mine are not.

*

You say
When you put your ear to me
You can hear the ocean

'I would meet you upon this honestly'

I think
I am flotsam on which you cut
Your foot while wandering.

*

I am fret full of rich tapestries
and those in them
and those who commend them
and those who just look
That a stitch worried
frays the whole
But done with straight hand
impossible to undo
My scissors are blunt with
cutting other people's threads

*

in airports
i am home

Owen Sheers

Feeling the Catch

It is four in the morning, and one lamp strobes me in its
stutter,
the only sound, its filament fizzing, popping, fizzing
as last night's rain slugs by in the gutter.

I am by the pub where things happened first:
the hot flush of whisky down the back of my neck,
the quick release in the alley out back.

There is a body shifting on the step of the doorway,
deep in its sleeping bag, a draft excluder caught the wrong
side;
a dirty blue chrysalis of dreams and cold.

But all I can think of is the heat in there,
the press of dancing bodies, the sheen of sweat,
piss streaming in a full ceramic sink,

three men round it, looking down, hands in front,
like picketing workers round a brazier
or bowed head mourners at a funeral sermon.

And of Dai, doing his flaming Drambuies,
head back, eyes to the ceiling, mouth open wide,
singing hot notes of blue flickering flame.

How he used to make us lower the match
that lit the pink, ribbed roof of his mouth,
before it caught and he felt the catch;

a flame from nowhere,
hot on his lips, which he would shut with a snap,
careful not to burn himself on his own blue breath.

And then his gasp, his long outward sigh,
and the shake of his head, like a horse,
bluebottles caught in its eye.

*

And now here, on this hill, where I came with you,
the girl in the red dress whose name I can't remember,
on the only night we ever spoke.

Lying back on the bonnet of your father's car,
watching the house lights strike off,
shrinking the town to its tight centre.

Then looking up, constellations growing on the night sky;
following the curves of slow satellites
or the quicker release of meteorites: eighteen that night.

I never did see that dress, or you again.
Some told me it was because you were with Dai,
although I never knew and you never said,

but I still like to think I made an impression,
or at least left a reminder in the shallow dent
in the finish of your father's car –

right where it's hardest to beat out.

*

This was where Dai came too, eighteen that day,
Stopping above the valley's river of lights.

Unscrewing the cap like a bottle of squash,
and pouring it over his thighs,

lifting it, so it ran, thick over his head,
hair slicked down, an otter rising through water.

Then he must have lowered the match, careful,
waiting for the quick release and the catch,

which when it came set his body alive with fire,
flames quick at his finger tips, hot on his lips,

peeling at his skin, turning his hair to magnesium strips,
which fizz, the pop, then fizz.

The car windows shatter,
shooting stars out,

glass constellations growing on the dark tamac
with each pane's crack and burst,

while Dai, head back, mouth open wide,
burns himself on his own blue breath.

Unfinished Business

We often saw him pass the classroom window,

bunking off, jumper alive with ferrets,
two thin dogs snapping round the hem of his coat.

At fifteen he bolted from a tattoo parlour,
down on the docks in Swansea;

bursting into the light before the tattooist could start the S,
sprinting down the street, ATAN still bleeding on his head.

He tried to make sense of it in biro.
appearing at the gates, the crucial letter scratched in,

and despite our fear (we knew he'd dropped
a breeze block onto some bloke's unconscious face,

attacked a teacher with a Stanley knife, threatened
to fill in his kids and fuck his wife) we still laughed;

though it was always he who provided the punch lines –
usually ten or twenty times before someone could drag
                                                    him off.

The Blue Book

"**Blue Books, The** (3 vols., 1847). Reports published by the Government on the state of education in Wales… the Commissioners reported that the common people were dirty, lazy, ignorant, superstitious, deceitful, promiscuous and immoral, and they blamed all this on Noncomformity and the Welsh Language." – *Encyclopaedia of Welsh Literature*

Lingen, Symons and Johnson,
their names give them away,
holding thumb-cornered text books,
not a word of Welsh between them.
Page or man.

They found their God spoken in words
that ran unnaturally in their ears,
and they wrote their decree.
Rather silence than these corrupt tongues,
the words of the father shall not be passed on to the sons.

*

Because this is how an empire is claimed
not just with stakes in stolen land,
but with words grown over palates,
with strength of tongue as well as strength of hand.

*

And now another blue book
this, my brother's school book
(bill-postered with bands, but blue beneath)
and inside, the Welsh in his and his teacher's hand.

It has fallen open on a half-written page,
The space beneath hos work shot across with red pen:
Pam nad yw hyn wedi ei orffen?"
"Why is this not finished?"

Well, maybe it is now, if not in me, then in him,
my brother, ten years younger,
but a hundred and fifty years and one tongue apart.

When You Died

I ran to the top of a hill
and sat on its broken skull
of stone and wind-thinned soil.
I watched the Black Mountains darken
and the river slip the grip of the town.

I went to the pond,
the one in the field above the house,
its borders churned to mud by the cattle.
I thought of how we skated there,
taking the risk, despite the sound of the ice,
creaking like a boat's wet rigging.

I went to your house,
and saw the long, low chicken sheds.
I remembered your voice behind me,
as I, afraid of the sudden peck,
stretched my hand into the dark
to take the warm eggs, one of them
wearing a feather.

Mrs Frazer

Once a day, Mrs Frazer, eighty years old,
goes snorkelling on the reef,
which lies like a secret beneath
the dark waters across the road.

She enters in her dress, finding no need for any unpeeling,
or showing of flesh;
she prefers to let the cloth billow about her,
until she floats, face down, in an impression of death.

Sometimes, to swim through a wave,
she will spin on to her side,
but mostly, she just lies still,
resting on the swollen stomach of the tide.

Skirrid

I. Facing West

She is a she, but I do not know why.
This hare-lipped hill, this broken spine of soil

that stretches across my window
steep-sided, a sinking ship.upturned.

Where I stood at Easter,
the Black Mountains shifting their weight in the west,

breathing their storm towards me,
turning a slow cloud down their shoulders

that came to me with hail-shot, straight in my face.
Ant eggs blown in my hair.

II Facing East

A kestrel tilts on the breeze,
over swollen fields, deciding in the sun,

a dark scales paused in the sky,
hanging in the balance,

until it folds and dives, a falling grain,
and is no longer there.

Only the view is left, and in the distance,
the Severn, a long haze

which flexes once a year,
rolling one huge wave down the estuary.

Now though, it is quiet, deciding,
its muscle still growing far out at sea.

Owen Sheers

You go on ahead
i.m Oliver Smith 1980-1999

Years later, and you went on ahead once more,
just the two of us, riding bikes now not ponies
over the winter mountain towards the reservoir,
a dark promise in the valley's fold.
Where we had ridden those ponies until they swam,
water-trotting, sea-horse necked, their weight like a threat
beneath us,
not sinking, not floating, but holding
that space of in-between they did so well.

Not like you, who didn't do half-way
but were always the one to go on ahead,
like then, in front, the inter-woven trails
of your bike's wheels, long spiralling lines of dark DNA
imprinted in the snow,
until you took a jump too far, and fell –
your back tyre skidding in a perfect arc,
cutting a dash of black through white.

It was what I should have read, that mark, that day,
black on white.
It told us what perhaps we all secretly knew.
That you would always go on ahead,
wouldn't wait and stick around.
That someone like you, with your head burning orange,
could only ever burn so bright for so long.
That you'd soon take that jump too far,
that leap beyond the in-between,
and stub yourself out, leaving us behind, waiting,
in the quiet afterburn of who you'd been.

Not Yet My Mother

Yesterday I found a photo
of you at seventeen,
holding a horse and smiling,
not yet my mother.

The tight riding hat hid your hair,
and your legs were still the long shins of a boy's.
You held the horse by the halter,
your hand a fist under its huge jaw.

The blown trees were still in the background
and the sky was grained by the old film stock,
but what caught me was your face,
which was mine.

And I thought, just for a second, that you were me.
But then I saw the woman's jacket,
nipped at the waist, the ballooned jodhpurs,
and of course, the date, scratched in the corner.

All of which told me again,
that this was you at seventeen, holding a horse
and smiling, not yet my mother,
although I was clearly already your child.

Viki Holmes

Lantivet Bay

the country lane unpins its hair
a bend in the road tangles
the rearview mirror
with speedwells and campions
but you can drive me
anywhere you like
and never mind the sunshine
and the flowers

footpath's steep to the shore
where we tumble
and the slow drift of sand
to the first erosion of our love
we touch each other in the cliff's shade
wanting to be cut off
but nor ready for high tide yet

and the damp-towelled shuffle
to the carpark
like walking on pebbledash
but sharper
like a lollystick
against the playground wall

home and showered
my belly button clean
of sand and you
I slip outside the house
and run my hands
over the plaster
wanting
that rough cold
to feel again
those indents on my skin

Pornography

tall as he was
bent almost in half
to sup from his glass
at the table's edge
I should have been watching the band
he was

instead I stared at his lips
mouthing the words
through a small smile
I shouldn't have seen

the song was a good one
1977 again
the band authentically ugly
that night we were back
with the Pistols and the Damned

it was like hearing it for the first time
I wanted amphetamines
and pogo-ing
but spying him across the room
nodding to the singer
lips in sync

I felt as though
I'd crept into his bedroom
and watched him get it on
with his first girl

Viki Holmes

Living room

we sat wrapped up like wombles
in blankets and bad armchairs
you with a mouth like crushed fruit
me counting the handspans between us
even then

we were the tesco value family
with our open-plan breakfast-bar
bargain-basement flat
light slid through the letterbox slit
but no more than that

we weren't ready for it
that slip into adulthood
and somehow
along the way
we forgot that love was there

like the tv in the corner
we never used
or the heating we thought
would cost too much
to ever turn it on

Miss Moon's Class

my news book says
yesterday I cut myself
on a blade of grass
I drew a whole field
at the top of the page
a thousand green sticks
blood on my finger
and a big smile

my head's only just higher
than the grass
but my smile's bigger than
Babylon

Hushabye

another bare-kneed summer
bottle-blonde lashes and the day's end
half-asleep
not used to early shifts
she dozes through Pontprennau
misses all of Newport Road
face flushed against the window
nodding, nodding
then she slides
and jolts
as the bus
shifts
gear

it's a small thing
a stranger's breath
at the base of her neck
it's probably the wind, she thinks
and smiles and shifts back
in her seat
not moving then
'till the bus
pulls in

Coming down

seventeen and slumped
in a nightclub toilet
turning a cigarette packet over
(you can see what they're thinking)
and over
(no, really, you can *see* what they're *thinking*)
when the woman with hips like castanets
clicks up to the mirror
and pouts like you wouldn't believe
you're leaking giggles everywhere
all over the cigarettes all over the floor
when a voice snarls from the cubicle door
I DON'T KNOW WHO'S LAUGHING
BUT THEY'RE GOING TO GET HIT
so you run back out to where
mirrorballs bounce off red walls
and faces don't fit their owners
dodge the strobes
with a smile like an elastic band
and navigate the stairs
every step's a shift
until you land where you began
in three dimensions

I'll meet you in The George

what I looked for
was the quiet in your heart
the words uncalled for
springing from cool lips
that said you weren't for me
I'd come too soon

your smile curved up
to brush my fingertips

too close a touch
with you so far away
I left you there
can't leave the memory

that feathered sharpness
of your grave bent head
as fag smoke coiled in blue
among the beams
a yellow jukebox
coughs up love's old song

I have become an expert

at kissing quietly

inhale/exhale a breath timed
to match another
and we're too polite to mention
that love resides
in the back of my throat
a half-chewed fishbone

give me some help here

a blow to the back
for the winded baby
let me cough it up onto the carpet

give me some help here

give me a living room love
something I can hand around
with the sandwiches
something
my mother can know about

Hilary Llewellyn-Williams

Making Landfall

One morning you wake to a difference
in the touch of the air:
somewhere a door is open

the smell of the world comes in
and flutters round you
as if stirred by wings

as if borne your way on a shore wind
to the deck of your narrow ship
after months at sea –

an imprint of what waits below the horizon
beyond the grey expanse
cold heave of water

to reach you now, coffee and motor oil
fresh flowers and new-baked soil
warm rub of concrete

an onrush of green, an invasion
of leaves and spices:
a tang of sweat follows

and the world arrives and immediately begins
to reassemble its forms
out there on the edge of sight

On such a morning you notice the birds
the shapes their bodies make
in free flight.

Animaculture

The gardening angels tuck their robes
into their belts, pull their boots on,
cover their heads with haloes and set out

to cultivate the world. Each one
has hoe and sickle, spade and watering-can
and wings, and a small patch

to care for. They come in all colours:
dawn, rain or dusk, rose, marigold,
moss, midnight; gliding between

reflections, rarely seen. At three
years old, occasionally I'd catch
the flick of a wing, a glitter on the air

a tickle of warmth behind me, someone there
playing roll-in-the-grass with me
pushing my swing. And at night

my gardening angel laid her head
beside me, smelling of daisies,
and breathed with me. At my maiden flight

along our street, my feet grazing the privet,
past lamp-posts and garden gates, her voice
in my head steered me and said –

This is the way to heaven, along here.
Since then, so many false choices:
knotted with weeds, I'm overgrown

and parched as dust. Who will open
the door to the garden, who will water
me now? Wise child, I trusted my own

right words, I knew the angel's name,
and that death was part of the game.
I find it very hard to remember her.

The gardening angels prune and propagate
moving in secret through the soul's acres;
have I called on mine too late?

Whistling, she strolls in from long ago,
And she hands me the rake and hoe –
Your turn, she says, and I feel my wings stir.

Letter to my Sister

It is summer where you are, but I am cold
as I write this, and my house is dark all day,
and the garden soaks up rain like a black sponge.
You will spend Christmas, you say,
trekking the mountain roads and the coast paths
with that giant man of yours. I picture you
lean and brown, frowning into the sun,
shouldering your pack with the supple grace
I loved. I can see your face
clear as light, open as day: sunshine
is true to you. The flowers are strange
where you live, they speak Maori names
like the knock of wood on wood;
the birds crack words in your primeval trees.

I catch a dream of you, and here it is,
your blue note through my door. Pressed
in the thin folds like a paper flower
you wave to me, you sound your brand-new vowels
inflecting to the page-end, quick and small.

I look for more of you, and raise my eyes
to the far edge of the world. Down there,
beneath the roar of oceans, where the stars
make different shapes, where summer is,
lives someone that I knew in the cold wind
that blew along my shore. And as I turn
towards the sun, so she recedes
into the dark. My sister in the skin,
circling with the earth, keep good your seasons.

from The Tree Calendar

Ivy
September 30th – October 27th

In the dawn fields, white fogs lie breathing,
        making a Chinese landscape:
the Nine Kings of the North Pole descend.

Cattle shifting in the near distance
        sidle away from winter;
step by step, it has surrounded them.

The trees look thinner in this long sun:
        drawing their juices in, they
contemplate dark traceries of mould.

Brown and gold brushstrokes over the hills.
        A smell of frost and woodfires;
ivy increasing as the leaves fall.

Flowering ivy for the late bees
        full blown and glossy, tightens
its massive grip, defies the cold Kings,

keeping slow but certain purposes:
      enveloping the whole world
in patterned mounds of vegetation.

Here is a ruined cottage, sprouting
      leaves, snake-stemmed and rustling:
part of the woods now, splitting apart.

The roof gone, how can the structure stand?
      Ivy has loosened its knots.
Stone by stone, it is undone again.

From a roost above the fallen hearth
      an owl calls in full daylight:
the Nine Kings of the North Pole descend.

But they step down from whatever heights
      they journeyed in, with keen joy,
trailing blue air, a ripened sun.

There is a large fruit, still uneaten.
      Look through a crack in the door.
Nine Kings treading ivy on the floor.

Hawthorn

The river thick with rain
pushes against its banks

and glides like heavy silk
smoothing the boulders

Each shoreline packed with trees
outdoing one another in bursts of green
in white bloom froth and foam

over the rushing water
all jostling together
There on the far side
rolled and drifted into a still pool

the body of a sheep bright as hawthorn
caught in the leafy shallows

the olive runnels

Fallen in surrender its head down
and smothered in the river

that passes with the sound of soft thunder
the rising pulse of summer

The Seal Wife

One day I shall find my skin again:
my own salt skin, folded dark, its fishweed stink
and tang, its thick warm fat, great thrusting tail,

all mine: and I'll take it and shake it out
to the wind, draw it over me cool and snug,
laugh softly, and slip back to my element.

I shall find my stolen skin, hidden by you
for love, you said, that night the sea-people danced,
stashed in some cleft in the rocks where I dare not go

but used to go, and dance too, stepping free
in my new peeled body, the stalks of my legs in the moon-
light strange, my long arms shaping the sky

that have narrowed their circles down
to the tasks of these forked hands: lifting,
fetching, stirring, scrubbing, embracing – the small

stiff landlocked movements. In the sea
I plunged and swam for my own joy, sleek and oiled,
and I loved at will in rolling-belly tides.

Here love is trapped between the walls of a house
and in your voice and eyes, our childrens' cries;
whose boundaries I've understood, a language

learnt slowly, word by word. You've been dear and good

how you would sing to me, those wild nights!
- and oil my breasts by firelight, and dip down

to taste my sea-fluids. I'd forget to mourn
those others then, trawling the flickering deeps.
Now I cry for no reason, and dream of seals:

an ocean booms in the far cave of my ear
and voices tug at me as I stand here
at the window, listening. Our children sleep

and by daylight they run from me. Their legs
strong, their backs straight, bodies at ease
on solid ground – though they play for hours on the shore

between sand and sea, and scramble the wet rocks
gladly. It won't be long now, the waiting:
they love to poke and forage in the cracks

of the cliffs; sharpeyed, calling, waving.

Steering by the Stars

Nobody steers by starlight any more:
we're too clever for that

we've packed the stars away
in the dusty dark

turned the key in the lock.
Eyes down, we study our instruments

measuring our location
without benefit of heaven

the beasts above us, the ones
with fiery faces

blotted out by light.
We have banished night from the world

who needs it? It belongs
out there with the past

with the star names
of the Magi, who saw

the eyes of the Bull and said:
Aldebaran. Elnath.

Dubhe they said, and *Alioth*
and *Albaid*, the haunches of the Bear.

From the East, a long slow caravan
sets out across the desert

ships navigate the wastes
of the open ocean

and in the empyrean a blaze
of beings journeying

along with them, and Pegasus
is beating his four wings:

Scheat, Markab, Algenib, Alpheratz.
Heroes of old, the Archer

his bow stretched *Nunki* to *Kaus*
and the Hunter with the jewels

in his belt: *Alnilam,*
Rigel and *Betelgeuse* and *Bellatrix.*

In our age they glimmer wearily:
the Hunter with his dogs

Sirius and *Procyon* is redundant
eating burgers, watching Sky TV.

But the old names still resound
like incantations, syllables

of power. Just say it: *Acamar* –
a breath of incense on the night air.

Here are the citadels and palaces:
Alphecca, Al'Nair

Zuben'ubi, Tower of Justice.
Ankaa, the burning Phoenix.

And then the warriors:
Kochab, Polaris, Menkent, Rigilkent

conjured from their strongholds
in the hills, armed with their scimitars –

Schedar. Shaula. Enif.
The fixed stars. They flash crimson

gold and purple, sapphire, emerald.
They spin and twirl, coming to life, pulsating –
we're being watched, the pressure of their gaze
stinging our scalps like rain.

And now the summoning-spell
the words of sorcery:

Mirfak. Denebola.
That's when we all look up.

Biographies

Tiffany Atkinson Berlin-born, has lived in Wales since 1993 when she came to Cardiff to pursue research in critical and cultural theory. Now a lecturer in English at Aberystwyth University, Tiffany teaches critical theory, contemporary literature and creative writing. She was winner of the BBC Radio Young Poet of the Year Competition in 1993 and 1994, the Ottakar's and Faber Poetry Competition 2000, and the Academi Cardiff International Poetry Competition 2001. She has had poems published in *Poetry Life*, *Sampler*, *The New Welsh Review*, *Poetry Wales* and *New Writing 11*, and is currently working on her first collection.

Deborah Chivers has recently completed her PhD, and was, until May 2002, a creative writing tutor at Cardiff University. She is putting together her first collection of poetry, which includes many that have been published individually. She writes short stories using the name Deborah Davies, and has had her fiction broadcast on Radio 4 and published in MsLexia magazine. She was a prize-winner in the last two Rhys Davies short story competitions.

Sarah Corbett grew up in north Wales. She won an Eric Gregory award in 1997 and has an MA in Creative Writing from the University of East Anglia. She has published two collections of poetry: *The Red Wardobe* (Seren 1998) and *The Witch Bag* (Seren 2002). *The Red Wardobe* was shortlisted for the Forward and T.S Eliot prizes. Her poems have been translated and widely anthologised. She currently lives in West Yorkshire with her young son and is completing a third collection of poems and a screenplay.

Lyndon Davies was born and brought up in Cardiff and has lived in various parts of Britain and France. His poems have appeared in *Poetry Wales*, *New Welsh Review* and *Fire* and he has also written a series of essays on poetry and art for *Poetry Wales*. He is currently living in Llangattock, Powys.

Rosie Dee originally from Bristol, now lives and studies in Bangor, and finds her inspiration in the dark skies and low light of the Snowdonian landscape.

Alexandra Duce-Mills has lived and worked in various south Wales valleys for the past 10 years. She has been published in *Poetry Wales*, *Planet* and *New Welsh Review*. She was awarded second prize in the John Tripp Award for Spoken Poetry in 2002. She has produced a CD entitled *finding things* in which she performs her poetry alongside a backdrop of music from found sounds such as a squeaky wheel on a climbing frame in a London Park. She is currently working on a further CD in collaboration with other musicians.

PC Evans is a poet and freelance translator. Originally from south Wales, he has lived in Amsterdam since 1990. He has published poetry and translations with *Leviathan Quarterly*, *Poetry International* (Rotterdam) and *Poetry Wales*. He was featured in 'In een ander licht', an anthology of contemporary Welsh poets published in Holland in 2001, edited by Robert Minhinnick. He was also a co-organiser and translator of Seren's definitive anthology of contemporary Dutch poetry, 'In a Different Light' (2002). His first collection 'The Unreal City' was published by Headland in 2001.

Cliff Forshaw was born in Liverpool and now lives near Bethesda. Between leaving school at sixteen to work in an abattoir and completing a doctorate on Renaissance literature at Oxford, he did a variety of jobs in Spain, Italy, Germany, Mexico and New York. Recently, he has taught Creative Writing at the University of Wales, Bangor and for the Open College of the Arts. He has published four collections of poetry and a fifth, *Verb Sap,* is due from The Collective Press. Poems and translations have appeared in the UK, USA, India and Australia and in the British Council *New Writing* and Forward Prize anthologies. In 2002 he won the Academi's John Tripp Award for Spoken Poetry.

David Greenslade is from the village of Cefn Cribwr, and now lives in Cardiff. He has many books of poetry, prose and non-fiction in print, including a novel Celtic Hot Tub (Gwasg Carreg Gwalch). He works for the Open College Network and has received scholarships from the British Council and the Welsh Arts Council. He writes in Welsh and in English and his poems have been translated into several languages. His most recent collection of poetry, *Weak Eros*, was published by Parthian in 2002.

Richard Gwyn was born in Pontypool and has lived in Cardiff since 1990. He has published five collections of poetry and prose poetry, most recently *Walking on Bones* (2000) and *Being in Water* (2001, both Parthian), and is currently working on translations of poetry from Spanish and a novel, *Woman in the Night*. He teaches creative writing at Cardiff University and is Poetry Editor of Parthian Books.

Graham Hartill Born in the Midlands, has lived on and off in Wales since 1971. Studied and taught in the USA and China. Two Arts Council of Wales Writers Bursaries and a Scottish Arts Council Writing Felllowship. Co-founded Lapidus (writing in health-care). Countless workshops and many residencies, currently working as *Lifelines* facilitator with the Ledbury Poetry Festival. Apart from several of his own collections, he has published adaptations from the Chinese, notably *Ruan Ji's Island/Tu Fu In The Cities*, (Wellsweep Press). *Cennau's Bell*, his selected poems, is due out in 2003 from the Collective Press.

Viki Holmes was born and brought up in St.Austell, Cornwall. She has lived in Cardiff for the last four and a half years, and in 2002 completed a degree in English Literature and Welsh at Cardiff University. She has worked as a tour guide in a restored Victorian garden and as assistant manager and licensee of an Italian restaurant. She also knows how to operate a paint colourising machine, but currently works for the International Baccalaureate Organization's languages section. Her work has been published in *First Time*, *Poetry Wales* and *The Yellow Crane*.

John Jones trained in electrical engineering with the Ministry of Defence but resigned during the eighties to work as a stockman in the Black Mountains of Gwent. He farms now above the market town of Abergavenny and is a member of Longtown Mountain Rescue Team. He was awarded an Arts Council Bursary for his work on 'containment theory' and his most recent book 'Carreg Las' has been much acclaimed. He has recently been described in 'The Journal' as the best practitioner of 'white space' known today. Check out his web site www.blackmountainpoet.com for a greater insight into the man and his art.

Patrick Jones was born in Tredegar and educated in Oakdale, Cross Keys and Swansea. He is a poet and dramatist, author of *everything must go*, (UK Tour, March, 2000), *the guerilla tapestry; poem for the gone world* (film for BBC Wales, 1999) and *unprotected sex*. His new and selected works, *fuse*, is published by Parthian (2001).

Hilary Llewellyn-Williams now lives in Pontypool, but for many years lived in West Wales. She has published four collections of poetry with Seren, most recently *Greenland* (2003) and has read her work in Britain, Spain, New Zealand, Canada and Portugal. She has recently been collaborating with the composer Ian Lawson on a musical setting of her sequence *The Tree Calendar*. She has tutored several times for the Arvon Foundation and Ty Newydd, and until recently, taught Literature and Creative Writing at Cardiff University.

Lorna Lloyd was born in rural Essex of Scottish, Irish, Welsh & French ancestry. She married a Welshman, settling permanently in Wales in 1984. Lorna studied Fine Art in Nottingham and Graphic Design/Illustration at University of Wales College, Newport (1st Class Honours) and has worked in the arts for many years. She currently works as a freelance copywriter/designer and part-time tutor at UWCN. Winner of the Poetry Digest Competiton in 1995, she has performed her poetry widely and been published in *Poetry Wales*, *New Welsh Review*, *Planet*, *Iron*, *Poetry Digest*, and many small magazines. In 2002 she received an Arts Council bursary to concentrate on her first poetry collection.

Lisa Mansell was born and bred near the sea in Porthcawl, South Wales. Her poetry affirms her love of the sea and the significance of place. Lisa's poetry is also guided by the sound and music of words, which are often accompanied by images of classical music that have been made important to her by her experiences as a viola player in a symphony orchestra. She now lives in Cardiff, and has recently graduated with a BA in English Literature from Cardiff University. She will soon be entering an MA in Creative Writing at Cardiff University.

Mike McNamara is from Larne, Co. Antrim, but has lived in Wales since the age of eight. He has worked as a lorry driver, scaffolder and labourer, and also as a magazine illustrator, potter, scrap dealer and soldier, during which time he experienced life as a military prisoner for nine months in Colchester. As well as writing, Michael is also a songwriter and lead singer with one of south Wales' most popular groups, the ten-piece Big Mac's Wholly Soul Band.

Tôpher Mills left school at 16 to work in a factory, followed by a number of other occupations from roofer to stand-up comic. He founded Red Sharks Press, works on radio and television and has written columns for the *New Welsh Review* and the *Western Mail*. He has performed his work widely in Europe and the USA and is the author of several collections of poetry, including *The Dancing Drayman*, *The Bicycle is an Easy Pancake* (the title poem of which has become a cult item amongst French velophiles) and *Swimming in the Living Room*. Tôpher Mills is a member of the Welsh Academy and was Chair of the Welsh Union of Writers between 1997 and 2001.

Annabelle Mooney was born and grew up in Australia and attended university there and in Glasgow. She currently lives in Cardiff, where she works as a researcher in globalisation and the communicative aspects of HIV/AIDS. She is also a jazz singer and actress, taking the role of Titania in the summer 2002 Everyman Theatre production of *A Midsummer Night's Dream* at St Fagan's.

Kate North was born in Kirkentillock but brought up and now lives in Cardiff. She gained a BA Honours from the University of Wales, Aberystwyth in 1999 and an MA from the University of East Anglia in 2001. She is currently working for a PhD at Cardiff University in Critical and Creative Writing. She has appeared in numerous magazines and anthologies and is a regular performer at poetry events in and around Cardiff and London. She also spends time running a popular arts event in Cardiff. Her work has been described as a 'garish cabaret of fondant images' by the T.L.S, and she was short-listed by Forward last year.

Pascale Petit was born in Paris and grew up in France and Wales. She has published two poetry collections. Her second, *The Zoo Father* (Seren, 2001), is a Poetry Book Society Recommendation and was shortlisted for the TS Eliot Prize. It won an Arts Council of England Writers' Award and a New London Writers' Award. In 2000 she was shortlisted for a Forward Prize for Best Single Poem. Her first collection, *Heart of a Deer* (Enitharmon), appeared in 1998. She co-edited the first Poetry School anthology, *Tying the Song* (Enitharmon, 2000). She trained as a sculptor at the Royal College of Art, has travelled in the Venezuelan Amazon, is poetry editor of *Poetry London* and a contributing editor to the US magazine *Rattapallax*. Her poems have been broadcast on BBC Radio 3 and 4.

Kerry-Lee Powell was brought up in Antigua, Australia and Canada and moved to Wales in 1987 where she went to university and drank with Welsh poets for many years. Her poetry has appeared in various magazines and anthologies. She was given an Arts Council grant to write a novel 'The White Buffalo', which she is still writing. She lives in Canada at the moment, where she works as a DJ.

Steve Prescott Cardiff born builder and wedding singer. Poems published sporadically in various magazines and anthologies. A small collection will be published in 2003. He has taken part in many readings in various parts of the country and has had poems published in *New Welsh Review*, *The Yellow Crane*, *The Bristol Anthology*, *sampler* and *Ramraid* amongst others. He lives with his partner in Canton, Cardiff.

Lynne Rees was born and brought up in Port Talbot, and has lived in Kent since 1985, where she teaches Creative Writing at the University of Kent. She received an MA in Writing from the University of Glamorgan in 1996. Her work has been published widely in literary journals and appeared in three previous anthologies, including *Teaching a Chicken to Swim* (Seren, 2000). She has read her work on BBC Radio and at The Poetry Society and Troubadour Café in London. In February 2002 she became the first Writer in Residence at Benenden School, Cranbrook.

lloyd robson is a poet & prose writer whose texts spill over into typography, photography, visual art & performance. he is also a workshop tutor, occasional event promoter and recovering journalist, but is no longer such a pain in the arse. his prose poem, *cardiff cut* (2001) and his new collection, *bbboing! & associated weirdness* (2003) are published by parthian.

Cecilia Rossi was born in Buenos Aires in 1966, educated bilingually, though Spanish is her first language. She studied Law at the University of Buenos Aires, trained as an English teacher, completed an MA in Creative Writing at Cardiff University (1997) and is now working on a PhD in Translation Studies at the University of East Anglia. She has won several translation prizes in competitions organised by the British Centre for Literary Translation.

Rhian Saadat originates from south Wales, although her childhood was spent in Germany and Cyprus. Her writing is influenced by time spent working in the Middle East, and later, in southern Spain. She moved to Paris in 1990, and joined the writing group at the British Council, run by the late Douglas Oliver, and Alice Nottley, completed the MA at East Anglia in 2000, and is currently studying towards a PhD. Her poems have appeared in several anthologies and literary magazines. A first full collection of her poems is due to be published by Parthian.

Owen Sheers was brought up and educated in Abergavenny, south Wales and New College, Oxford. A graduate of the UEA MA in Creative Writing he was a recipient of an Eric Gregory Award in 1999 and winner of the 1999 Vogue Talent Contest for Young Writers. His first collection of poetry *The Blue Book* (Seren, 2000) was short listed for the Forward Poetry Prize 2001, Best First Collection and the Welsh Book of the Year 2001. The *Independent on Sunday* named him in the Top Thirty young British writers and his first prose work, *The Dust Diaries* will be published in the UK by Faber & Faber in autumn 2003, and by Houghton & Mifflin in the US. He currently lives in Cardiff where he works as a freelance writer and broadcaster.

John Short was born in Liverpool, of Irish, English and Welsh ancestry. His work has appeared in two previous anthologies: *Poetry North* (Forward Press, 1998) and the *Liverpool 126 Anthology* (1998). John also writes under the name of Hubert Tsarko, and plays the bouzouki. He lives in Athens.

André Stitt is an internationally renowned performance artist. Originally from Belfast, he lived for many years in London, and currently heads the Time Based Art department at the University of Wales Institute, Cardiff. He has worked as a live artist since 1976, producing hundreds of performances at major galleries, festivals, and other sites around the world. André has also made three CDs of his poems in collaboration with musicians, and is the subject of diverse critical writings and interviews, most recently *Small Time Life* (Black Dog Publishing, 2002) and *Homework* (Krash Verlag, Cologne, 2002).

Ifor Thomas was born in Pembrokeshire. He was a Founder Member of Cabaret 246, Horses Mouth, Working Title Writers - all performance based writing groups, and has tutored poetry in performance at Arvon, Totleigh Barton and Ty Newydd. He has performed at many venues including Hay-on-Wye literary festival, Newport Festival, Swansea Festival, Cardiff Bay Lit, Apples and Snakes, Tunnel Club, London. He has won the John Tripp prize for spoken poetry and been runner-up twice. His new and selected poems, *Unsafe Sex* was published by Parthian in 1999.

Chris Torrance was born in Edinburgh but has lived in Wales, in the Upper Neath valley, for as long as anyone can remember. For twenty-five years he led a ground-breaking evening workshop for writers in the Extra-Mural Department of Cardiff University, attended by several of this anthology's contributors. He has performed in his poetry and music band Poetheat since 1985, and has been widely published, notably by Paladin in *The Tempers of Hazard* (1993), alongside Thomas A. Clarke and the late Barry MacSweeney.

Zoë Skoulding grew up in East Anglia and taught in India before moving to north Wales in 1991, where she teaches English in a comprehensive school. In 1994 she launched *Skald*, a magazine for poetry and prose, which she continues to edit. Her first collection, Tide Table was published by Gwasg Pantycelyn (1998) and her work is included in the Seren anthology Oxygen (2000). She has been, and is currently, involved in several musical projects, as bass player, lyricist or spoken word performer.

Landeg White was born in south Wales and has taught in Trinidad, Malawi, Sierra Leone, Zambia, and England. Among his various books are studies of V.S. Naipaul, of Mozambican and Malawian history, and of southern African praise poetry, together with five collections of poems. His translation of Camões's *The Lusíads* won the Texeira Gomes prize for 1998. He is married with two sons, and lives in Carapinheira, Portugal where he teaches at the Universidade Aberta (Open University). His *Where the Angolans are Playing Football: Selected and New Poems* is published by Parthian (2003).

Samantha Wynne-Rhydderch grew up in a naval family in Newquay, Ceredigion, where she first started writing. Her first full-length collection *Rockclimbing in Silk,* was published by Seren in 2001. She lives in Newquay, works in Oxford and sails in her spare time

Index of Titles

Index of First Lines